GAME OVER

Love, Sex & Adventure

Without Playing 'The Game'

John Cooper

INSERT COINS TO CONTINUE

First Printing – 2015

1 North Rd, N7 9HD,
London, United Kingdom

CONTENTS

Foreword

There is a wealth of strength and power within us all, and the way to access it may be surprising. Only the weak and desperate are forced to take without giving, yet so many of us interact with others this way. You want approval. You want the girl to think you're funny. You want your boss to be impressed. You're told you need to 'Game' them. You feel like you constantly need something from others. But you're wrong. They need something from *you*.

Game Over is a roadmap out of a self-made prison. When it comes to the social world, no one is naturally weak and desperate. We can all summon a vast reservoir of strength and value with a simple yet tragically elusive mindset—that of unconditional giving.

Game Over is aimed directly at the pick-up artist community—a sub-culture, a sub-world for men trying to learn how to become better with women in the context of dating, attraction and sexual connection. If you know nothing about 'PUA' or 'Game', as it's also called, then you will still be able to follow my story, as what I break down in this book is typical of our results-seeking society.

I tell the story of how I went from being a lil' pipsqueak at school who had no love from girls, to becoming the party boy who had no troubles with women, to then getting dumped by my first love and then falling head first into the sordid world of pick-up artistry. Then actually becoming worse with women than I was before, despite mastering all the tricks.

Had I have not had the experience of being a genuine natural before, I would have thought Game was developing me. That's why I have a very unique and important perspective to share with you, because most industry coaches say that they were bad with women but achieved success only after learning PUA (Game).

Most men look for the easy solution, the 'life hack' that produces maximum results from minimal effort. PUA methods of meeting women offer this, and thousands of men have blindly subscribed to it. If you tell men who don't believe they are naturally attractive enough to attract the kind of women they want, that there are tricks and techniques they can learn that can fix that, of course they are going to sign up.

Game Over explains why the PUA industry and community will ultimately hold you down into a nerdy boy's club, focussed on hunting for women which ironically repels you from women and creates more suffering. I explain how this is not to be confused with a framework to improve one's life, including around women romantically. I deconstruct PUA and explain why it's flawed and stems from unresolved childhood abandonment issues.

Then I show the paradigm shift into **Social Heartistry**—which inverts the context of Acquisition to **Giving** (unconditionally, from a healed heart). From working *for* a woman, to **Playing** *with* women. Moving from neediness to **Autonomy**.

These 3 core principles are a gateway to total social freedom and accessing limitless creative potential, because they navigate you to become, what I call **The Social Artist** (no, not the pick-up artist!) The true artist does not copy anyone, he has his own unique style and identity, he doesn't care what people think of him, and is never defeated, because he expresses for himself. He doesn't force anything and doesn't fixate on any particular outcome and it's for that reason that the Social Artist is always winning and always the most attractive person in the room.

Your journey as you read through this book, will most likely be undoing all the pick-up stuff you learnt, addressing your pain and become your own Social Artist, who is free from conflicts, free from the shackles of the PUA prison and able to create powerfully with everyone around you.

Overall, there are 4 completely new chapters in this edition, and I've consolidated a few chapters from the first book to make it read a bit more fluidly. I've also removed a lot of the references to pop science, neurology, any language which sounds new agey, or anything that could possibly muddy the waters.

I've also updated the homework exercises at the end of each chapter which I've taken from the **UltimateDatingProgram.com** which is an online academy I've spent the last few years filming and putting together with Sean Russell from Menprovement.com, where you can be taken through the entire dating process and watch me demonstrate everything in this book, in real life social settings.

So, with all that being said, let's get straight into the heart of it…

Prologue: Game Over

Is pick-up and the 'seduction community' making you feel like a creep? More and more anxious and distanced from women, while you keep trying to hunt them? Well, I know how you feel man; I've been there.

But I'm lucky enough to have escaped. I feel liberated, fulfilled, and life-giving. I invite women into my life. I certainly don't 'approach' them, 'acquire' them and take, take, take. I don't do any of that. My relationships with myself, my friends and the women in my life are genuine. And yes, I have an abundance of amazing women in my life, even though I don't do pick-up. Shocking, right?

Now, first off, I don't like the word 'seduction'. Look it up. It means "to lead astray". It also seems a bit sad and pathetic for someone you meet to say, "Hi, I am a seducer, I seduce women", as they curl the side of their mouth and nonchalantly raise an eyebrow.

My definition of seduction is an experience that's shared between myself and a woman—an encounter that is led decisively by me but is co-created between the two of us. Certainly not a strategy to fill the hole in my heart of inflate my ego before I go looking for my next fix.

No. There's no more of those cocaine highs and lows of a pick-up addict. I am free.

But it wasn't always like this. I confess. I've been deep, deep down that pick-up rabbit hole. So embarrassingly far down it, I once struggled to see the surface. Sucked in by all the promises of Game, I would get worse with women, despite the mini victories that I used as a way to cloak my downfall in hope. Instead of Game, let's call it what it is—*hunting*. Even so-called 'natural' or 'direct' Game is still just hunting, acquiring and taking. Pushed on by an army of pick-up gurus with abandonment issues deeper than any rabbit-hole.

But then I found a way out. How? Well, it certainly wasn't easy. Ultimately, by healing my broken heart and returning to purpose and balance, I managed to get out of *The Game*.

Yeah, there is a way out. You *can* live a beautiful life of integrity, attracting women and amazing people into your life wherever you go and you can do this all without the need to implement creepy strategies, tactics and controlling behaviour.

In this book I'll be outlining the paradigm shift from pick-up/Game into a new way of presenting yourself to the world.

Think of the sun for a moment. The sun gives unconditionally. When you start to come from this place of sun-energy rather than the vampiric energy of a black hole, you empower yourself to the point where you actually begin to feel like the sun. When the sun beams out a ray of sunshine, it doesn't demand anything back. If someone gets a suntan, that's all good. If someone steps in the shade, the sun isn't going to be 'rejected.' The sun just keeps on giving.

However, the acquisition-based intention of pick-up and Game is like a black hole. You've got to feed it. If you don't, it consumes itself, and you in the process. But, like I said, there is a way out of this vampiric pick-up paradigm and I want to show you how.

5

But before we begin, let's make one thing crystal clear: If you're looking for snake oil tricks and manipulation strategies to try to get your dick wet, close this book now, because this isn't for you. Also, if you're thinking this is 'Game 2.0' or the next evolution of the 'community'—you couldn't be more wrong.

Human attraction and intimacy existed long before a magician in a silly hat kicked off the pick-up community many years ago. The entire hunting & acquisition model of getting laid is seriously, seriously harmful. Pick-up in all its forms messes up how you see the world and how the world sees you and there is no way it can evolve, no matter how 'natural' it becomes.

What I want to communicate is a whole new perspective. A way to live with passion, playfulness and purpose that goes much deeper than the 'approach', 'seek', and 'destroy' mentality of Game.

Of course, this perspective includes sex and adventure with women, but when you live your life from this place, women become a bonus rather than the sole objective. You'll find deep fulfilment in areas of your life besides women. You'll no longer be desperately hunting women, yet you'll be attracting them into your life way more easily.

This way, women are no longer seen as 'targets' and objectives but lovers and friends.

After going through the pain, frustration and addiction of Game, and seeing so many good men get sucked into it, it's time to transcend Game once and for all—its language, its concepts, its duplicity and its harmfulness. It's Game Over, and not a moment too soon.

The clients I've taught are now using my new perspective to take off their pick-up goggles and truly reconnect with women without fear and without the need to hunt. I'm here to guide you out the adolescent wastelands of pick-up... Are you ready to take the journey with me?

Player One Has Entered the Game

Before I get into this, let's make this clear—When I talk about pick-up/PUA, I am including ALL types of 'Game':

Day Game, Night Game, Old- Skool Game, New-Style Game, Inner Game, Natural Game, Direct Game, High Energy Game, Low Energy Game, Real Social Dynamics Game (that pretends to not be all about Game, but really is). ALL GAME!

This might sound surprising to you 'natural' and 'direct' Game lovers out there, but as you'll see in the next few chapters, natural and direct Game are just another room in the same mad house and just as harmful to you, because at the end of the day, it's all the same thing: Game.

I'm not trying to dissuade you from taking action with women. Far from it! I want to show you how Game is driving you away from women, making you worse and worse with them. There's a simpler, more effective, less painful and infinitely more fulfilling way to express yourself here. In doing so, will help you become much more attractive—not just to women, but to all manner of people you meet in life.

Since 2009, I've been slowly infiltrating the pick-up community—like an antibody within a virus. I established myself as a coach, now I'm subverting the system into a platform for genuine high self-esteem, self-healing and self-expression. No longer will the seduction industry money moguls extort thousands of pounds off poor dudes to teach them how to out-manoeuver and disarm their 'targets' on their boot camps. I will teach you a new level of integrity and purpose to be carried forth in every aspect of your life.

So, let's start with my story: the weird winding road that drew me into the strange, sordid world of pick-up in the first place.

Midjohn

Here's the first big shocker. As a kid at school, I didn't get any attention from girls. But it didn't really matter at primary school, because the girls had 'the lurgy' anyway, right? I was always small growing up. I mean really small. My mum was so worried about me that she took me to see a growth specialist to have my wrist X-rayed. They worked out that I was going to grow to 5'10". But no one including myself believed it at the time, and I was offered drugs to boost my pituitary gland and accelerate my growth, which I refused.

Being Lilliputian in size didn't really matter through primary school, but when I hit secondary school, it was kind of a big deal. Once the residual pre-pubescent games of bulldog and hide & seek wore off, it was girls that mattered. And they were all we could think about.

Suddenly, the funny little pipsqueak with the bowl haircut who made everyone laugh was a hindrance to their chances of pulling girls. And I was kicked into touch, going from being an 'inbetweener' to the lower echelons of the nerd crew, where I festered quietly until the end of school.

Surprisingly, by graduation I had shot up nearly a foot and was average height but by this point the damage was done. My reputation was tarnished, and a fresh start promptly required.

When I left to go to 6th form college, no one knew me as 'Midjohn' (midget + John) anymore. I had a new lease of life. I could be the cool kid and for the first few glorious weeks I was. I grew my hair out and strutted down the corridor in my Black Market Records Mk2 bomber jacket, doing the ghetto 2-step handshake with the other cool guys.

Girls were *actually* interested in me.

Disaster Strikes

It all fell apart as over a freak couple of months, my skin rapidly broke out into such full-on acne, that there were more custard-filled spots than actual clear skin on my face. I had to use my mum's concealer make-up pen. It was normally used to conceal the odd blemish but now I was using it to colour in my entire face until I began to resemble some kind of poor man's Dale Winton.

My skin was so bad that I went into KFC and instead of serving me; Mohammad the chicken-vendor-turned-dermatologist-expert began lecturing me on spot creams. In the end, he talked me out of buying the Zinger tower meal and my stomach shrunk along with my self-esteem, again.

I was right back in my shell. Finally getting over being the short-arse and now becoming the elephant man's little brother. I had to go on liver drying tablets called Roacutane, with pills the size of an apricot stone. After four months my skin cleared up considerably, but I had to stop months before the end as it was giving me depression and sleeping problems. For the next few years, my skin had deteriorated back to square one and I felt that a life of celibacy was the only thing on the cards.

As I entered my early 20's, my skin naturally started to clear up. I had become a decent looking guy and girls were starting to give me the eye. In clubs, they kept falling into me on the dance floor. At that point I should have known to pounce, but I was still the small, ugly spotty duckling at heart. When girls kept falling back into me and hovering close on the dance floor, I eventually put my hands around their hips and suddenly, we'd be kissing. So, I reverse engineered the process. I started to position myself close to the hot girls around me on the dance floor and simply put my hands on their hips and it worked more often than not. I became rather proficient at it. It would go something like this: arrive from behind, put hands on hips, bump'n'grind for 30 seconds, rotate them 180 degrees, grind some more whilst cheek to cheek, feign the kiss the first time to ramp tension. Then go in for the real kiss, snog for a bit, then dash off onto another girl. I wouldn't say I'm particularly proud of it, but I kissed hundreds of girls doing this and learnt how to be very playful and tactile with girls, whilst not really knowing what I was doing, except for a little trial and error.

Sick on the Dancefloor

I became a big-time clubber in my 20's and stepped it up from the apple Hooch drinking, meat-market student parties transforming into 24-hour house music raves on the weekends. Our tribe of hedonistic adventurers would start off on a Saturday evening and 3 or 4 after parties later would finish Monday morning—with no sleep and no food in-between. It became a religious act that whilst buzzing my tits off, to be sick on the dance floor. It became a running joke.

Much like Doc from Back to the Future, when he slips and bashes his head on the bathroom sink to reveal the idea for the flux capacitor, I'm now hunched over my carroty celebration one night and it hits me; I'll create the sickest party in town, with the sickest music, the sickest atmosphere. It would be called 'Sick on the Dancefloor'.

Because I was very much in the jugular vein of the London underground clubbing scene, I knew the sound people wanted to hear on a night out. The current scene was good, but they failed to maintain the dirty, menacing electro- synth sound throughout the night. I knew the atmosphere people wanted—relentless hands in the air music. They wanted killers, not fillers. So, in 2006 I launched a trial night: an after *after* party for all those zombified clubbers who wanted something more, when everything else had finished by midday on Sunday.

10

On Mother's Day 2006 at 2pm in the afternoon, in a bar in the suburbs of London, I opened the doors to the first ever Sick event. Although only 30 or so people turned up, it had a great house party feel and everyone was bouncing off the walls by the end.

At the next party, 80 people turned up. The next, 200. By then I had to move to bigger venues in the centre of London. The party was now being talked about on Pete Tong's Radio 1 show and eventually, the event was pulling in 2000+ people at some of London's biggest venues.

Hosting on the night, swimming in-between the sea of clubbers, checking-in on the front of house, the DJ's, the sound engineers, the security—I'd greet the clubbers, share a joke or two, enjoy the odd kiss with a girl, then have to dash off and continue the night. I was hooking up with girls, but they weren't the objective, the night was. I was there to make sure it all ran perfectly. The girls, like I mentioned at the start of this book, were simply a side effect.

Whilst running my events, I also attended university in the north of England to do a graphic design degree. After resisting any kind of monogamy up to this point (I tended to get bored very quickly), I found my first love. She was the Snow White type and as she entered the room, little bluebirds would chirp around her.

It was a sort of schmoopy-poopy love, where we skipped down the road together and held each other's hands so tight that our knuckles went white. We couldn't even bare sitting opposite each other in restaurants as it was too far away. So we pretty much sat on each other's laps. Yep, we were *that* couple.

All Gone Pete Tong

In my 3rd and final year at uni, I had a series of catastrophic events, with my cousin dying, and having to live with a drug dealer and a thief. I would come home from my studies and find my housemate wearing my leather jacket and jeans, and the kitchen table covered in phones he had stolen from girl's handbags on a night out. Not to mention the painkillers and sleeping pills I took to drown out the noise of the nightly house music that pumped through the walls on either side of my room, as the doorbell sounded all night with people coming to buy coke.

Plus, while I was head-down trying to pull off my degree, back in London my event company 'Sick on the Dancefloor' was being hijacked along with all the accumulated door money from two so-called friends who registered the brand as a Ltd company behind my back.

Miraculously I pulled off a first-class honours degree and won an award for my art directing work. But it was at the cost of my relationship.

"You're working too hard" I now realise meant "you're not spending enough time with me". It was a stressful time, and I was finding sex a chore. When she came to my house in nothing but French lingerie under her coat, and I couldn't bring myself to even raise a smile… that spelt the end.

I really needed time to myself—some cave-time to process everything, yet she required lots of attention, and any hesitancy in the affection between us, was being perceived as a lack of commitment.

I could feel the breakup coming and almost felt like suggesting it myself. But still, I was so cut up when I was finally on the receiving end of it, I went back to my mum's and spent two weeks locked in my bedroom, seeing and speaking to no one.

When I finally hauled myself out the house, I went to a bookshop, initially looking for books on the theme around "how to get your ex-back". Instead, can you guess what book I found?

Yeah, you got it—*The Game* by Neil Strauss.

And so started my journey into the hocus-pocus world of pick-up.

Chapter 1 – Falling for the Pick-up Industry Hoax

Initially, I bought into the whole pick-up thing. Hook, line and sinker... rod and copy of Fisherman's monthly! For any of you that don't know what pick-up is, it's a global community forged from the book *The Game,* which tracks the hero's journey of a bald, squeaky-voiced bookworm called Style who goes under the wing of different Pick-up Artists ('PUA's') and miraculously becomes unstoppable with the ladies, like his primary mentor called Mystery—a freak show, furry-top-hat wearing magician-type who has broken down his seductions into an Aspergers-style formula, geared around controlling women with a maths equation.

Like most people who read the book, I stopped reading halfway through and indulged in the manual half of the book. I failed to take the time to read the second half where Straussy explains how only after he left pick-up and returned to being a normal dude again, got the girl of his dreams.

But it was too late. I was hooked on the idea of using these irresistible manipulation techniques to get any girl I wanted. Go back to being a normal dude? Fuck that, I've got 'sniper negs' to pull off with 'HB9's' yo! (That reads like fucking gibberish, doesn't it?)

So then began my quest. I was still reeling from the pain of losing my girlfriend. My friend Nicky Mabbs was coming round to bring me Nando's in bed. I was so bad, my skin was going yellow. If you haven't seen it already, go and watch the movie Swingers, where Mikey is picking up the pieces of his broken heart. Much the same, I cried myself to sleep every night for around 2 weeks.

"John, try to turn a negative into a positive," said Nicky, repeatedly. And I thought, that if I can't have the girl of my dreams, then how about this as a consolation… ANY girl, ANYTIME, ANY place! That's it—I'll become the best PUA in the world! That's a pretty good substitute for not having the girl of my dreams. I can fucking do this.

Nearly every sport I had ever taken up, I had reached a high level in a short period of time—county squash player, Arsenal youth footballer and junior golf captain of my club. I was a high-achiever when I put my mind to something. So this pick-up sport would be no different. I knew this was it. I was gonna smash it.

I went through 'Mystery Method' and lapped up all those magic bullets PUA's were talking about. I quickly gravitated towards other 'wingmen' who I had recognised on nights out by over-hearing them use the secret lingo! I was quickly going out 'sarging' with them (an overused pick-up term for seeking girls) and we would critique each other's performances.

My favourite line was the 'canned opener': "Hey do you think it's ok for a guy to wear women's jeans?" directing my attention to the 'obstacle' and not the 'target' of course.

There would be a burst of initial energy and in pick-up terms I had 'spiked the girls buying temperature'. But after starting off so well, I could feel the energy dying. The moment things go silent it's over, I thought. I needed more ammo...

'TRANSITION!' my friend whispered firmly in my ear, who strategically stood in my shadow. *But what the fuck's a transition?*

"Urrr, how do you two know each other?" I stammered. "Phew!" This had kept things going a bit longer, but the energy had certainly dropped a notch or two.

Shit this is dying...

"You're the good girl and you're the bad girl," my friend declared, triumphantly striding in like Lord Flash Heart from Blackadder to 'save the set'.

The energy shot up again and the girls giggled, looking puppy-dog-eyed towards my friend. This is what a good wingman is for, to step in when the energy is dying, right?

I thought back to when I was a kid. I remembered playing balloon kick-ups, keeping the balloon in the air to prevent it from touching the floor. Now I was at a point in conversations where I was trying to keep the energy of the conversation airborne and prevent it from touching the floor, at which point the conversation was over and the "hey, I better get back to my friends" line would inevitably be uttered.

My 'openers' were strong, but my 'mid-game' sucked. I needed more 'chick cracks' to keep the conversation going and to successfully achieve 'C1'—comfort building, according to the three-tiered model

(attract, comfort, seduce) pioneered by Mystery and friends during the genesis of *Game*.

16

In order to reinforce my artillery with new ammo, I went away and did a palm reading course. Now when I was with a girl, I could take their hands and do a reading on them. My newfound weapon was executed perfectly when I was in Pizza Express and I got up from my table, walked around the restaurant and 'opened' girls who sat on different tables. My friends watched in amazement as I had girls throwing me their hands, goopy-eyed.

Man, I'm getting good at opening, but I wasn't successfully building comfort, I thought. So, I went away and did a cold reading course by a guy who taught Derren Brown. Now I was able to talk to girls and drop alarmingly accurate cold reads so that they were weeping into my shoulder.

On the surface I looked incredible. I could 'open' the whole top deck of a bus and come away with a hoard of numbers from nearly all the girls. I was 'opening' hundreds of girls and 'locking myself in set', 'sniper-negging' the 'target' (pointing out an insecurity or dropping a tease to level the social statuses), and working the 'obstacle' (dealing with the unamused friend who stands in the way).

I knew the material inside out, including 'rolling off' to save value, and doing a 'takeaway' when I pre-empted the energy dropping. I was proudly teaching my friends and had built up such an arsenal of pick-up material that I started my own PUA group on meetup.com to regurgitate all this.

Then I realised…Shit, I hadn't actually had sex once since doing all this stuff. But I reassured myself that it's probably just a settling in period of internalisation. So, I ploughed on, learning more and more theory. I was consuming information at an insane rate.

So long as I learnt more, eventually I would reach the Promised Land, or so I hoped.

17

Despite knowing all the theory inside out, I was still hitting a brick wall. Despite the occasional bumbling lay, I was a shell of my former self, and even worse than back when I was Midjohn.

I needed to up the ante. So, I went away and did an NLP practitioners course. Neuro-linguistic programming is a popular route for the PUA looking to ramp up his control strategies on women, by anchoring emotions into words, controlling and creating sexual frames, and other Ninja-like techniques to get past her defences.

As I dug deeper, I found more advanced ways to manipulate and control outcomes. But all the time I was getting worse with women, and feeling less and less connected to them.

"I don't get it", I said to my best friend Tom.

"I used to be such a natural. Remember when I ran my parties or even when I just used to go out and hit the dance floor, it's as if they'd just come to me. Like I was made out of Velcro".

It took Tom, who knew nothing about pick-up to spell it out to me:

"John, take everything you've learnt, put it in a box, get out there and just let things play out. Go back to being John again".

But I couldn't do that, the very thought of that was frightening.

"No way man, I wouldn't be in control".

"Bingo, just try that then…" he replied, grinning.

Letting Go

So I went out and whilst my sarge buddies were nervously positioned on the bar, with sweat glistening from their predatory brows, beer clamped to their midriffs, analysing the room and working out their openers, I was just chatting to everyone around me. Guys, girls, waitresses, bar staff. Soaking up the night and harmonising with it, spreading a web of energy around the place as I grooved to the vibe. I went back to the attitude of being the event organiser, who wanted to connect the room to my great party.

What a relief. I felt joyous and lighter in my body. I could hear the music more than ever. I was smiling and dancing again. A huge monkey came off my back. I felt connected to the room, and more importantly, to people again.

I spin round and there's a girl there. I'm having fun and extend that fun out to her. I start a dance-off with her before playing some more. We laugh and tease each other, before falling down onto a sofa together. We chat, playfully bat each other in response to each other's banter and then have a playful kiss before we jump up to rejoin the party—because the party and the vibe was the important thing here.

My former 'wings' come rushing over to me, aghast.

"Holy fuck dude, what was your opener? How did you transition? What was the kino you just did?"

This was baffling to me. *"I didn't open her man, or transition!* We were just playing around!"

"Yeah you did—we saw you. Did you use an opener about her dance moves?"

"Haha na man, I didn't use any opener..."

"Yeah you did, we saw you... what was your comfort builder? You locked her in on the couch, and micro-isolated her, don't lie to us! You kiss closed! You fucking kiss closed!"

A light bulb was going off in my head. We were now out of sync. They were seeing the interaction through the pick-up goggles, and I was just seeing the interaction as the **side effect** of the fun I was already having. There was no strategy or control, there was no pick- up. I had surrendered and was letting things unfold naturally.

I spent two months just going out and dropping all pick-up methods and all attachment to outcome and the funny thing is, girls were coming back into my life again. I distanced myself from my pick-up wings and just went out with my old friends who went out to have fun, yet still enjoyed female company. I was sexually attracting again and making meaningful connections.

At the time I saw this as just a lucky break. I had a glimpse of freedom, but I was still lured by the endless promises of *The Game*. So I fell back in. This time, much, much deeper.

Slipping Back into the PUA Trap

Looking back, I should have continued that relaxed, natural way of being, but after so long I decided to rejoin my PUA wings, as they were the ones that seemed to be taking the most action and engaging the most with girls but as soon as I was back within their energy— back within their collective intention on a night out, I found myself locking up and paralysed. It was my turn to 'cold approach' the 'set' next to me. I couldn't do it. A huge wall of adversity hit me. I panicked. I felt separated. Useless. I felt like an 'AFC' ('average frustrated-chump') which is PUA lingo for the regular, unenlightened, sexless, non-PUA men of the world.

"Hey man looks like you got serious 'Approach Anxiety' tonight. Warm up with opening a 'base set' first and remember the '3-second rule' next time you 'approach'. You'll be fine", uttered one of my wingmen.

This used to be obvious PUA advice but it felt jarring. I mean how else do I talk to girls, if I'm not 'approaching'? But now, it felt wrong—seriously wrong. It suddenly all became so much hard work again, but I didn't really know why.

So I decided to confront my anxiety and battle it head-on, like trying to stare down a bull as it charges. I began belligerently cold approaching girls. Thousands of them—more than ever. Fuck it, I was determined to master pick-up, blast through the anxiety and hammer through the adversity.

My friend Labi and I would set each other harder and harder challenges. Whilst on holiday in Turkey, I told him to sit with two girls in a restaurant. He would tell me to jump into the taxi, which three girls had got into, and drive off with them. The challenges got harder and harder, to the point where Labi got me to approach a couple holding hands in a candle-lit restaurant and hit on the girl in front of her boyfriend. We had become fearless PUA Robotrons.

I had memorised so much technical theory that I was now proudly telling people I was a PUA, but I wasn't genuinely connecting with these girls, and this was a splinter in my mind. But I thought, "Hey, it worked for Straussy so maybe I just need to learn more. Maybe it's time I pluck up the big bucks and do a PUA bootcamp..."

And so, with this next fatal stage of thinking, I jumped with both feet onto the PUA merry-go-round...

Academy Exercise

Welcome to the Academy Exercises section of this book. These will follow each chapter, and the idea is to bring concept into reality as you unplug from Game to become more authentic and recover your social skills.

For the first exercise, I want you to have a think: how did you first fall into pick-up. Was there a painful experience before it? Write down this painful experience now. Be honest with yourself. Was it a break up, death? Perhaps a feeling of inadequacy, or isolation that was unbearable? This will be important for later.

UltimateDatingProgram.com

Chapter 2 – The Pick-Up Circus: A Trip to Pleasure Island

STEP RIGHT UP, STEP RIGHT UP... IF YOU WANT ALL THE WOMEN AND ALL THE SEXUAL FREEDOM IN THE WORLD THEN YOU NEED TO COME TO PLEASURE ISLAND...

So, motivated by the loss of my sweetheart, I went deeper and deeper down the rabbit hole. I even gave myself a PUA name: 'Trend'! What a cunt! But the cold truth was; I wasn't getting better with women—I was getting worse. A LOT worse. More social anxiety, more frustration and more cock-in-hand.

I had fallen victim to the self-perpetuating marketing machine that is The Pick-up Artist Industry. But of course, like all willing initiates, I was blind to it.

I had created my own avatar name for myself, surrounded myself with 'sarge buddies' and had access to the best pick-up material out there. Surely everything was in place for a utopia, right?

But most significantly, I had internalised *all* the PUA concepts, which I believed was the secret code to a woman's knickers. But the ironic thing is how that was exactly what was keeping me confined to a theme park where only the house (yep, the PUA industry) was winning. Because we know the house always wins.

There's a great scene in the Disney movie *Pinocchio* that summarisesit well. An old cackling man whips the horses, as he leads jovial kids into Pleasure Island on his wagon. Once in, the little whippersnappers fire off from theme park ride to theme park ride, smoking, drinking, smashing up the place and generally creating absolute mayhem. Jiminy Cricket is running around shouting "there's something phony about all this" as he watches everything unfold. Then the big doors to the fortress are shut by the big dudes in black capes. After so long, in a harrowing scene, the kids start growing tails and ears and eventually transform into jackasses. Eventually they become slaves to the old man, destined never to leave the island.

Well, this is how the PUA racket works. Run predominantly by money moguls, these companies lured me in by preying on my insecurities with women, opening my emotional wounds, and then promising a sexual utopia. Once in, I was imprisoned by the circus, I mean *cough* community. The doors shut firmly behind, and my compatriots and I moved from one PUA YouTube video to the next PUA bootcamp in the hopes of making our big breakthrough with women.

Ultimately, some would get so frustrated that they chose to go on the super-duper ride with *Mr.#1 Best PUA in The World*!

Shortly after they parted with their thousands, they were back where they started, in search of the next big thing. Bouncing from wall to wall of the community, like a frustrated wasp stuck inside a lampshade.

After so long in the pick-up circus, I started to become someone I was not. Even at the point where I had evolved past using canned openers routines and pre-meditated lines and I was now using 'Natural Game' —I had *still* lost myself. I was viewing the territory like a battlefield and seeing a woman as the enemy. I had become a Pleasure Island jackass, like everyone else in the community, and was now a slave to the system.

In the movie, Jiminy Cricket finds Pinocchio and hurries him out to the top of the mountain and they have to, in layman's terms, get the-fuck-outta-there.

I didn't realise at the time, but the way I ultimately went back to attracting beautiful women into my life was by escaping this circus— as Pinocchio did and returned to being a playful, non-needy guy with a lifestyle and purpose, besides women. This didn't mean I had to stop maintaining my own principles of expressing my sexuality and creating playful and sexy encounters.

So, consider me the Jiminy Cricket of all this shit. I'm here to help you escape the circus before the doors bang shut.

Academy Exercise

Your next task is to stop reading and watching ALL pick-up material. You are going to stop following anyone who calls themselves a PUA or gamer. You are going to get out of PUA forums and drop all your wingmen. You are going to stop gaming. You are going to find friends who know nothing about PUA but love to go out to socialise and have fun. You are going to start weaning yourself off pick-up—starting right NOW.

UltimateDatingProgram.com

Chapter 3 – Becoming a Natural Gamer

At the time, I thought I had evolved by gravitating towards so-called Natural & Direct Game. This, I finally felt, was the Promised Land.

Natural Game, as you may or may not know, is often touted as a smoother, healthier, more advanced version of pick-up that PUA's gravitate toward after ditching their proverbial training wheels. So it made sense that becoming a 'natural' was the way to go.

In June 2010, I found a Meetup.com group called 'London Night School', claiming to teach men how to be naturals with women. The talks were held in an old classroom with a traditional blackboard, in an abandoned school in Finsbury Park, London. It was hosted by an enigmatic Australian 'man of mystery' Grant, who was only 22 at the time but had the maturity and presence of someone who had just circumnavigated the world.

Packed into the classroom, it felt like I had just become part of my own Fight Club but with horny blokes trying to pound pussy instead of each other's faces in.

Grant would give a couple hours lesson each week, on various topics like erotica writing, story-telling or personal styling and then set us all homework exercises for us to do, talking to women during the week. We would then arrive the following class and report back on our achievements or failures.

The whole time I was doing the lessons, I confess, I wondered why I was there at all, as I knew I was not a complete lost cause with women, but at the same time I didn't know what it was that had derailed me and made me lose all my mojo.

Grant's classes seemed to lack structure, with arbitrary topics thrown together and there wasn't a cohesive thread to tie it all together. There was no sense of being guided through each stage and levelling up. It was more a case of "here's a bunch of cool ideas, I'll throw it at you and you can make sense of it all".

Grant also used to contradict himself quite a bit. For instance, he'd tell us to read one new self-help book each week and then simultaneously tell us to *never* read self help books but to just burn them!

With that being said, there were some real nuggets of gold within what Grant taught, if you were deft enough at extrapolating them. Some that stick with me, even today. I've included a particular homework exercise Grant set me, on the **Ultimate Dating Program**, which you can see at the end of this chapter.

When Grant's 6-week course finally finished, I didn't feel as though I had truly 'made it'. I was still struggling to get back to my old self with women but I knew Natural Game *had* to be the way forward.

I asked Grant if he would personally mentor me and take me under his wing, like Mr Miyagi does with Daniel-san in Karate Kid.

Grant agreed under the condition that I find him three people to sign up to his next course…

I duly oblige and find three budding students who all paid up and Grant asks me to make the hour journey to meet him in a bar in central London…

"So John, I've decided I'm NOT going to train you".

No reason, no apology. Just—see you later.

Grant had given me a taste of Natural Game, but closed the door on it, and in a very snidey way. Feeling miffed, I remembered during Grant's lectures that he mentioned he worked with someone called James in Melbourne, who he referred to as "a skinny, scrawny little Kung-fu fucker, but one of the best in the world".

Scavenging online, I eventually found James! He wasn't just a one-man mystery in a hidden ghetto school room, but had a whole company dedicated to helping guys become Natural Gamers. He looked the part too, with his long floppy Aragorn hair and 5 o'clock shadow.

To my delight, he wasn't teaching the formulaic pick-up stuff of how to trick girls using lines or routines, or pretend you weren't interested, in order to somehow demonstrate high value. Instead, he was teaching techniques on how to project your intent when gaming them. As I watched his videos I could see a lot of what Grant was trying to teach us, but laid out in a much more linear and clearly explained way.

This was it! An opportunity to go deeper into Natural Game! I *knew* straight away this was my next step…

Joining the Madhouse

I reached out to James and told him about the coaching I had done in London with Grant and said I would do whatever it took to continue the teachings, as I was left half-baked. James tells me I'd have to wait, as he wouldn't be back in London for a year or so.

"No need! I'm going to fly out to Melbourne to see you!"

James later admitted he was blown away by this, as he agreed to let me fly out there to be trained up and brought into the fold.

"You'll be part of the madhouse John!"

When you hear that you think of a Playboy mansion—sex, drugs, rock 'n' roll, non-stop parties, snorting cocaine off some brasses' tits, orgies and general debauchery, don't you?

When I finally arrive in Melbourne, James is locked in his bedroom and going through a breakdown. There is a schizophrenic in the basement hooked on meth and a manic depressant in the other bedroom, who only left his room to smoke roll ups or DJ at the local pub. So, when he said madhouse... he genuinely meant it!

I am asked to help out with various jobs including the filming of his two day conference event, and I thought in return I'd get trained by all the coaches. Instead, James just hands me a camera and asks me to capture 'infield videos' of me picking up girls on the streets, with Liam, one of his coaches.

Liam was your typical Incel, nerdy Gamer type, who saw talking to Women as a World of Warcraft manoeuvre. I was confused as to why this guy was a bone fide coach, as the virginity seemed strong in him. It later transpired that he was occasionally getting laid but with the low hanging fruit, shall we say.

I suppose James didn't see the need to coach me or was going through too much personal shit at the time, so he just got me making content for his channel straight away.

I started filming these, including one I aptly called 'Rapid Escalation' where I 'approached' a girl on an escalator in a mall and would have her number in my phone before we got off at the top. I published this video on YouTube and everyone in the community loved it, but I felt too ashamed to follow up with this girl. Can you imagine dating her or even getting into a relationship with her only for her to see the whole interaction on YouTube a couple weeks later! Talk about killing the vibe!

I always found doing these 'infields' uncomfortable. It felt morally wrong and like we were taking advantage of the girls for the sake of YouTube views.

"But how else can we show other guys how to be better with women unless we do this", I used to rationalise to myself.

"This is the way you put yourself in the shop window as a coach." James would also remind me. But I felt like a prick doing them.

Academy Exercise

Go out and be completely 100% honest to 5 different women. (Mix this up with women you know and also strangers).

UltimateDatingProgram.com

Chapter 4 – Remembering The Art of Play

Whilst filming the 'infields' one afternoon, I pass a barista working in an outdoor coffee house and I stop by. Instead of 'approaching' and aiming to 'number close', as I had been doing all week, I decide to just let go and have a laugh;

Barista: "What can I get you?"

I look at the menu board...

Hmm... "Can I haaavvvveee... your phone number".

Even though I was asking for the number, as I was in the 'infields', I really didn't give a toss about her response, or the number. It was just a gag to amuse me and her and anyone watching the video.

Barista: "Haha. What, a guy off the street, I've only just met?"

I continue the gag: "Look, do I have to order a croissant with it!"

I'm now in a no-lose situation, where I'm revelling in the PLAY and I know anything that happens with this girl, I come away winning...

Barista: "Ok then...here it is" ...and she hands me her number scribbled down on a bit of paper.

A big light bulb was going off in my head.

I was technically doing everything I had done before when doing pick-up and 'approaching' girls and 'number closing', but this time the context had changed. The reward wasn't the actual number. The reward was the moment-by-moment PLAY.

Yet the funny thing was, I still came away with her number! Even if this girl was to say; "Get lost", it would have been hilarious and I still come away triumphant. I can't lose.

Ahhh, *this* is what I used to do when I was a natural with women, either partying or running parties! I'd be constantly PLAYING! Like when I told you the story earlier of falling back on the sofa with that girl and having a kiss then jumping back up to rejoin the party and my former wings aghast at how I accomplished it.

Through play, I can still take masculine action in the same way as pick-up, but there's now no rejection. I'm bullet proof. The more times I was playing with women, the more attractive I was becoming and the more of my old self was returning.

Even when girls would scoff and ignore me, it was almost like; "Haha what a boring girl!" Or "she missed out on *that* gravy train!"

Then ten minutes later she would be looking over at me wishing she could be part of the fun. Or joining me later on in the night, because she realised, she could have a much better time with me than any other guy in the venue.

Something strange was also happening. Whereas before I would see everything as winning or losing ('closing' or 'rejection'), it was as if that didn't exist anymore. Every time I was playing with girls and they didn't vibe with me, it was almost as if *they* looked rejected and silly.

I did more of the 'infield' videos but I had created a new identity for myself. My style wasn't about focusing on 'closing', but about how much fun I could have with the girls in that moment and what I could create *with* them.

I was no longer the Pick-up artist. I was the **Social Artist**.

I was getting into the habit of vibing and playing with the people in my environment and Liam filmed a hilarious 5 minute sequence of me walking through the mall...

I see a girl working in a bakery; "My, what lovely baps you have".

Then I immediately pass a girl with glittery red shoes on; "If you tap those together 3 times, you'll end up back at mine".

Then I see a girl working in Tie Rack; "Cracking rack you've got!"

The more fun I was having, the more invincible I was becoming. The more irresistible I was becoming with women again. The seal had broken and I was really swagging and back to my best.

It was like I had gone from being the serious actor on stage who has his entire set scripted out and rehearsed, back to becoming the quick-witted talk-show host, who is unprepared and improvising in every moment.

I had even resolved the earlier internal conflict over the filming of the 'infields' and now right at the end, I would do a little reveal to camera and let the girl know exactly what I was doing.

Such as The 'Double Day Game Close' video where I ironically get caught in the crosshairs of a TV reporter for a breakfast channel, stopping people on the street and interviewing them on... wait for it...

dating! (The irony). As she asks me the questions, I flip each one onto her and lay it on thick;

Her: "What's your ideal first date?"

Me: "Straight back to mine".

I go maximum flirt-mode and try and make her blush as much as possible on camera until the end of the interview when she says she has a boyfriend and I seamlessly move onto her friend who is holding the camera and ask her out!

"Hey, you know what. *You* were the one I really liked".

It was a hilarious video and the community loved it. I also felt good about showing my style in a way which wasn't creepy hidden camera footage, where I surreptitiously acquired a close, but rather showing what could be created in the banter between two people. Or in this instance, three!

I was getting my mojo back and I realised what had been fucking me up the entire time... Game.

Academy Exercise

You're going to do the same thing! When you next order your coffee or beer, you're going to look up at the menu, or at the various drinks on offer, and ask for their number. Are you rejected if she laughs and refuses? If so, what's changed?

UltimateDatingProgram.com

Chapter 5 – Transcending The Pick-Up Paradigm

Once sucked into PUA Pleasure Island, it can be very hard to see things from outside of the pick-up perception. You see, success with women occurs *outside* the pick-up world, not within it. You can't have fulfilment within the pick-up community. When I started telling people that, they were like "John, what are you talking about? How else are you going to be good with women unless you're practicing pick-up?"

But they didn't seem to realise, there's a difference between being good with women and being a pick-up artist. They're actually diametrically opposed. Just because you're a pick-up artist doesn't mean you're having connections and having sex, it just means you're *trying* to. If you do somehow manage to bulldoze a girl into bed, that doesn't necessarily mean you're good with women. (Harvey Weinstein anyone?)

Pick-up is like a madhouse. If you lived in a madhouse and all you knew were the four walls of that madhouse, and everyone in that madhouse said "this is normal" and all the teachers said "this is normal", when someone came along and knocked on the door and said "uh lads, this is a madhouse!" Then everyone in there would say *"he's* crazy!"

We've accepted the normalisation of the pick-up madhouse for so long that we think it's totally fine to assign strategic terminology to basic aspects of human interaction. That, to talk to a girl, we have to 'cold approach' the 'target' or when we're touching her arm, it's a 'kino-escalation'. Or we are curious and want to share ourselves with her, so this is the 'building comfort phase'. We've been in this madhouse for so long that we've forgotten it's just a game, and a very harmful one at that.

If you've ever seen the movie *Jumanji*, Robin Williams (bless his heart) gets quite literally sucked into the game and he spends so long in there that when the plucky kids come to rescue him, he has amnesia and forgets he's been in a game the whole time. Hunting infield and approaching his targets, he has become a survivalist. Eventually, he and the kids find a way to escape the game and return to reality. So why is it we can't see The Game we are stuck in and return to reality as well?

Pick-up as a Paradigm

This Game of pick-up is what I refer to as a paradigm. A paradigm is a specific framework of activity propped up by the beliefs, values and assumptions of the members of the community that operate within it.

The pick-up paradigm has been confused as a platform for improvement with women, within the context of sex and intimacy. There are seemingly no limits depending on how much of the material you consume. But the pick-up paradigm is built on a few extremely harmful and flawed assumptions, as I'll make clear in the next few chapters.

Pick-up promises 'success' with women and as you can see from my story, when I got into it, I assumed that after delving into it far enough, I would eventually gather enough of an arsenal of information, that the whole thing would internalise and then *BOOM*—I would be smothered in girls.

But what I now realise, is that pick-up actually puts men into reverse and they go further and further away from freedom and further away from connection with women.

That's because pick-up is actually, in itself, a very specific modus operandi governed by its own limited presuppositions. The mistake is thinking pick-up is an open and ever-blossoming platform to develop but it's not. It is impossible to be an attractive person around women and to develop genuine sexual and social fulfilment when you are still operating inside the pick-up paradigm.

It's the same thing as spiritually evolving oneself but only adhering to the very strict doctrines of, let's say, Scientology. Although there might be spiritual and moral concepts within Scientology, to go deeper into this paradigm to arrive at a place of spiritual freedom is only trapping you more into a belief system clogged with dogma.

A Paradigm Shift

Paradigms dominate the consensus of opinion amongst its members until someone comes along and finds anomalies that can't be answered by the system itself. The fundamentals are then challenged from the vantage point of a different perspective and a crisis occurs— a loss of faith. New ideas are welcomed as a way of stepping back out into the territory. As more of the community start to take on this new way of thinking, there is a tipping point and the new paradigm starts to displace the old one.

Foundations of a Paradigm

In this image, chances are you're going to see one of two things:

- An old lady with her chin tucked down

- A young girl looking into the distance

Can you see both of them? Imagine having seen this image and someone asks a question like:

"Hey what do you think the old lady's name is? What do you think the old lady has done with her life up to now? Where do you think the old lady lives?"

And with everyone answering this question, no one stops to question whether or not it's an old lady in the first place.

What pick-up has done is forced us into a one-dimensional way of viewing interacting with women:

"So what kind of *Game* are you into?"

"What are your best *pick-up* techniques?"

"What kind of *PUA* did you use to kiss that girl?"

It accepts and presupposes 'Game' as a constant, which traps the community into the 'old lady' paradigm.

So, if you keep evolving pick-up, you are only evolving that specific paradigm. You're trying to become good at pick-up, but you're actually becoming worse with women and with yourself, just like I was. (Despite the mini victories along the way, which trick you into thinking you're improving).

The good news is that although it may be hard at first, once you begin to shift your perspective, it'll become not only possible to see the reality of connecting with women without doing pick-up, but it becomes self-evident.

You will look back with fresh eyes and be in astonishment how you couldn't see it in the first place. Much like when you walk into a darkened room and turn the light on and see where all the furniture is. Even if you turn the light off again, you'll maintain an awareness of where the furniture is. You know it's there; you'll never believe the room is empty again.

What's at the heart of the pick-up paradigm?

In a word: Acquisition.

Academy Exercise

I want you to watch the movie Groundhog Day with Bill Murray. You will notice that once he realises he's stuck in a time-loop, he tries to engineer the perfect seduction on Rita, the TV producer he's in love with. After multiple attempts of cobbling it all together, he finally creates what appears like the perfect romantic moment.

However, every time he tries to push it further, he keeps getting slapped in the face. His routine and set of trusted techniques keeps failing at the last hurdle.

He even finds, that when he tries to recreate the sequence over and over again, it becomes more forced and try-hard. He is becoming more and more desperate and it's repelling Rita, despite him knowing the routine inside out.

Then, later in the film, he finally lets go of the need for Rita, and spends his days in god-mode, where he shifts his intention solely on helping the people of Punxsutawney.

He had shifted his intention from acquisition and seeking results, to one of unconditional giving, and as a result, breaks the time-loop and wakes up next to Rita, the next day.

Bare this in my mind when you read this book. We will discuss this more in the group on the program.

UltimateDatingProgram.com

Chapter 6 – Acquisition and the Work-Frame

The foundation of Game is *Acquisition*—the need to ACQUIRE women. This is the absolute, unquestioned and accepted law of Game. The whole pick-up framework is built upon this and 'getting' laid is the objective, plain and simple.

A fulfilling conversation in a bar with a girl isn't a success in the eyes of the PUA. In fact, it's a missed opportunity or a downright *failure*. Chatting to a girl you are intrigued by on the street, having fun with her and not 'closing' is also a failure. Even if a PUA coach applauds your novice efforts at conversing with a girl, the conversation is only seen as a baby-step towards the end goal of eventually getting her into bed. Only when we reap the reward of getting our dicks wet do we get the true PUA stamp of approval.

Sad, right?

This law of acquisition in the PUA paradigm is what creates, what I refer to as a Work-Frame.

The nature of work by definition is a process rewarded *only* upon completion. You work all week for a weekend, all year for a holiday, and you bust your arse off for a qualification at college. Those are all examples of working for an outcome. But guess what, you should never be working for women this way.

The reason we fall into a transactional Work-Frame with women is because we are conditioned by society to seek results and only when we achieve the result itself are we rewarded. This is then our 'success'. We then spend our entire lives chasing goals that we think will bring about our success and therefore our fulfilment.

Welcome to the turd in the punch bowl my friend. Welcome to the fundamental flaw in your perceptual reality if you choose to use the PUA paradigm or any similar worldview with women. It's the thing that is holding you back.

Any kind of activity within the framework of pick-up, like 'Day Game' 'Night Game' or 'sarging'—means the accepting of this Work-Frame intention and motivation of Acquisition.

Whether it's seeking numbers or seeking sex, they are forms of Acquisition and thus part of the Work-Frame. This is hard coded into the foundation of *The Game*.

No matter how much more super-duper, advanced pick-up material you consume, whether you choose a mechanical methodology using routines and scripts or follow supposed Natural Game, it's still pick-up. It's still Game. And it's still nourishing the inextricable core concept of Game: trying to TAKE.

It's 100% Acquisition and its Results are Based on Success or Failure

"What's wrong with this!? I want girls, so I work for the reward! We live in a goal-orientated world! Deal with it Cooper" **YouTube comment**

There is nothing wrong with actively expressing your desire to women and rippling that out to them but an Acquisition-based Work-Frame instantly creates a dichotomy in us. It makes us aware of our own emptiness—in fact it makes it resonate all the stronger and there's something *seriously* wrong with that.

Acquisition and emptiness are two heads of the same coin. The very moment you switch on your pick-up brain, you go into hunt-mode. You focus on results and use strategy to get results. Success and failure pop into play. You are lacking something. You need something. You need that damn result.

Specifically operating from Acquisition, fractures our holistic thinking and we instantly create the Work-Frame which is a binary outcome response of success or failure:

- Win or Lose

- Getting laid or Rejected

- Close or Blow-out

- Fulfilled or Unfulfilled

- Empowerment or Disempowerment

So of course, we place an immense value on the success part (closing) and condemn ourselves and those around us for not achieving (rejection). Success is high fives and pats on the back from our 'wings' and failure is 'rejection' and sympathetic pats on the back. We are an 'AFC' a 'beta male' or a 'loser'. Every interaction with a girl now rests precariously on this seesaw of doom—this win or lose, do-or-die scenario.

I'll be talking a lot about the power of language throughout this book, but you'll notice already how the PUA lingo reinforces a duality of win or lose on every part of the interaction, especially the key operational concept of 'rejection'. When operating from this concept, it drums in the Work-Frame and prevents you from enjoying yourself and being truly free.

- We see a girl we like and 'approach' her—she could respond well = WINNING… Or she could ignore me and I'm left with the cold shoulder = REJECTION

- We get into conversation and I ask for her number—she says okay = CLOSE… Or I ask her and she politely declines = REJECTION

- I text her later that day and ask her out. She says she'll meet me = WIN…Or I text her and she doesn't reply = REJECTION

- We go out in the evening and as I start to 'escalate' she tells me she has a boyfriend and she thought we were just friends = REJECTED… Or I touch her more and we become intimate = SUCCESS

- I take her back to mine and in bed and we fuck = SCORE or she won't let me 'bang her' = LAST MINUTE RESISTANCE = REJECTED

Through our Work-Frame and seeing everything as mini-goals to achieve—we create a punishment for ourselves if we fail achieving that specific goal. We then generate an increased fear of that happening again. (Approach Anxiety)

We become entangled in this toxic mess and all because we are obedient to the very fundamental of Acquisition that props up this Work-Frame paradigm.

Rats, Trapped in a Maze

To illustrate more clearly, let's take this example of rats in a lab maze; who are having their behaviour manipulated by electric shocks or 'punishments'. There are two possible channels for the rats to go down and if they go down the wrong one, they get shocked, until the point that even when the electrical equipment is taken away, they won't go down there anymore. Their minds have been reprogrammed.

Instead of being electrically shocked by a crazy scientist in a white lab coat, we instead shock ourselves with the self-inflicted punishment in the form of adhering to the binary Work-Frame concept of 'rejection'. These constant punishments have the same effect on our psyches as the electric shocks on the rats.

Because we are so opposed to being 'rejected' and feeling that ego-death, it leads to enslavement to the PUA authorities and their presented solutions to avoid this problem.

We try to avoid these painful feelings—not by dealing with it at the root cause and transcending the pick-up paradigm that creates this Work-Frame, but by going deeper into it.

Instead of learning to let go and interact with freedom, we go further into control and strategy, to guarantee that result. Just like I did in my early days when I ramped things up with NLP, palm-reading and cold reading courses.

As a result, we take on further programmed behaviour and this is what enslaves men into Pleasure Island, keeping them entrenched in the never-ending hunt.

Academy Exercise

Turn every transaction into an interaction (bus driver, shopkeeper, check out girl, barista, waitress etc). Instead of just ordering your drink or handing them cash, find a way to rehumanise it. It can be something simple as commenting on their name on their name badge or pointing something out about the lousy music being played!

UltimateDatingProgram.com

Chapter 7 – What Goes on Tour...

After just two months in Melbourne, I had got right back to my old self and had some incredible romantic adventures including getting with the celebrity TV weather girl and by the end of my two-month trip, I was pretty settled down with an amazing girl called Elise who was a doctor at the local hospital.

James must've trusted in my ability, because I was invited to coach a month later on his 10-day bootcamp across Eastern Europe.

We would start in Prague, then move onto Bratislava, Budapest, and then finish off in Split. The idea was to coach the students how to get laid in one of the Mecca's for hot women.

James had invited Sacha Daygame to coach—a wise-cracking, high-energy, bubble-gum pick-up artist, who looked like a dishevelled Wayne from Wayne's World.

Plus, Steve Mayeda—an amiable PUA veteran from Arizona, who had been in the industry since the beginning, and who I had already got to know online back in my early PUA student days.

We would start early in the morning and James would do a meditation with the students in the park and some kind of Chi Gong shit and then Sacha would take them out and get them doing zany social exercises on the streets like wiping bogies on strangers, to in his words; "Destroy Approach Anxiety".

I was deployed as the 'Night Game' specialist. Mainly because those environments came easy to me, and the other coaches were like a fish out of water at night.

The Angry Pitbull

It hits 2.01am in Club Roxy in Prague and officially I'm off duty from the first day of coaching. I didn't realise how much student jealousy I'd had, not being able to chat up the girls I'd seen and liked. I had to put my desires to one side. My time now though, I move straight to the bar, see a girl and shout;

"You're fucking tasty-as, you are. Come here".

I throw my arms around her and nuzzle her neck. She goes along with it playfully. It turns out she isn't just playful, she is absolutely shit-faced, and that's not my style, so I move across the bar and hit on a sexy girl in a skimpy black dress.

Now, I had no idea Steve Mayeda was filming. In fact, he was filming one of our students but caught the whole interaction in the background.

After 5 minutes of talking, I lead her to the other room to sit down but there is no couch. At first I'm annoyed. Seeing the lone chair, I sit down and yank her down on my lap. 10 seconds later, I hoist her legs up so she's laid across me. We kiss.

I look into her eyes and I say; "fuck it, lets go back to mine, c'mon".

"Maybe, let me have my drink". She replies.

I grab her drink off her and down the drink in one through the straw. She looks at me with contempt, but I know she's wetter than an otter's pocket.

"Cammon I've got vodka at mine", I say.

With that, I take her by the hand and lead her out where I wave a taxi.

We get back to mine, and she is absolute FILTH, telling me to spit on her and 'hurt' her. I consider doing 'The People's Elbow'.

She grabs the litre bottle of Evian by the bed, sticks it up her vadge and empties half of it into her. "Now suck it out" she demands, with a look of an angry pitbull.

I duly oblige. The taste of her from the inside is half fishy, half water, and is like licking cold puke but I carry on regardless.

After doing things that guarantees my place in hell, we break to smoke. I tell her to have it out the window, which overlooks our quaint, cobble-stoned side street. She sits on the window ledge, stark naked. It looks like a choreography of a Degas portrait. I join her in the window with my wang out and as people walk past, we shout "WELCOME TO PRAGUE!"

One couple walking past—stop and just stare at us for 10 seconds. I start to feel bad that I have offended them and their lovely neighbourhood. They then unzip each other's trousers and start masturbating each other, whilst looking up at us. After a minute or so, they then walk round the corner into an alley and we can hear them fucking.

For the first time in my life, I think I am speechless. I feel used, I feel cheap...But I fucking love it!

The next day, fresh from gaming on the streets, the students come up to me and ask me how it seemed so effortless for me the night before and why the girls seemed to be attracted to me and not them.

"I'm the ONLY guy in the club, NOT doing Game", I replied.

They looked at me the same way a dog looks at a crossword.

"But we saw you 'approach' that girl and 'close' her".

Much like my previous 'wings' from earlier in my story—despite what they saw and perceived, I wasn't doing Game. Even though, through their pick-up goggles (and perhaps yours) I was, but in my reality, during every point in that interaction I was never 'approaching', nor 'opening', nor trying to 'build attraction', nor was I judging the interaction on whether or not I was winning or losing at any one point. I had eliminated the 'Work-Frame'.

Even when I was leading her out the club, it *still* wasn't Game. And even when we hooked up, IT STILL WASN'T GAME.

Here's where guys get confused…looking back on that encounter the next day, if I wanted to, I could say "I picked up a girl last night", and it would be an accurate description of reality, in that context, but that does NOT mean I was actually DOING any 'pick-up' or running any 'Game' at the time.

No doubt as you read that, you're also having a hard time making sense of that, just as the students did, so don't worry. We've been metaphorically staring at the old lady for so long, we're not even aware there is a young girl there.

I've dedicated this entire book to explaining and articulating this different perspective and helping you make that paradigm shift. Hopefully, by the end of the book you too will be able to experience a bit of the same freedom and magic by completely detaching from Game, whilst still taking action and attracting beautiful women.

The first step to making that shift though, is to realise where things are going wrong, on the foundational level...

Academy Exercise

Learn to lead decisively, with total freedom. Start a conversation with girls by asking for a kiss or offering to take her home. Your mission is to purposely get rejected 5 times whilst doing this. Every time you get a 'No', you register it as a win.

UltimateDatingProgram.com

Chapter 8 – The Hunt, the Story, the Pointless Spiral of Pain

This foundation of Acquisition leads to an intention of seeking, grasping, or in pick-up terms 'approaching'—desperately looking for that thing. Acquisition leads to actions and activities resembling a hunt. You're hunting, plain and simple.

What is the Dictionary Definition of a Hunt?

1. The pursuit of capturing wild animals, regarded as a sport

2. The act of conducting a search for something

Now let's look at the pick-up 'sport'. Go to Oxford Circus, London on any Saturday afternoon and see all the huntsmen doing just this. They are lurking 'infield' on the streets, eyes narrowed, heads scoping out the territory, 'locking in' on their 'targets'. Waiting to 'cold approach' and 'disarm' 'sets', capture their prey or return back to their tribe with the prize of a number. It's the same bloody thing! It's a hunt.

It's not just London either. It is the world over, wherever the pick-up methodology has spread to.

Hunting, and living life in this way naturally creates a feeling of lack in us. The two go hand in hand. Hunting and lack. Hunting and emptiness. Think about it, the moment you decide "I need that thing", you have made a conscious decision that you lack that thing in your life, so now you need to cover the distance quickly and try and get it.

The danger is that the more we hunt, the more we reinforce this feeling of lack, until over time it builds from a vague feeling into a strong and deeply ingrained sense of emptiness which taints everything in our lives.

When we choose a path motivated by lack, we can't think about anything else except hunting and trying to get rid of that lack. We remain stuck in the gap between where we are and where we need to be. The crazy thing is, we created the lack in the first place with our decision to hunt, hunt and hunt some more.

Creating a Story of Pain

Emptiness and lack, for a few seconds, is mere a moment of unease. But when we force our body and mind to feel it over and over again this feeling grows, and becomes real. Oh yes, it starts to become us. It starts to become you. It unearths a deep wound and that lack in you becomes part of your identity and part of your story.

You see, every time you go out and say "I'm going hunting", which is what you're saying when you say "I'm gonna go do some Game", or "let's go pick-up some girls"—in that moment, you create that frame of lack. You drum it in deeper. And what happens if you do this every day and every night, week after week, month after month, into eternity?

Eventually, you have a story that is so big and convincing, you can't see the world any other way. You are immersed in this story, which is all about what you lack, and the pain it is causing. But you are the only source of that story, and it's time to close the book and burn it.

This doesn't mean stop meeting and having sex with women, in fact, when you stop hunting, you'll meet and connect with women far more easily. You'll realise more and more that you are already connected. You'll stop creating this artificial distance between you and women and take your first steps to becoming a genuinely attractive guy.

Never-Ending Pain

In that decisive moment when we decide to hunt something, we stop having it. We create a lack inside of us. We build this painful story from a deep wound in us, and then we go hunting to alleviate that lack, to cure that pain. It's a quick fix and the salvation promised by the hunt is an illusion. So even when we finally get what we were hunting—when we get that bit of tail, we get the result, but we don't cure the pain, we simply cover it up for a fleeting moment. The only way out is… you guessed it… stop. Stop hunting.

Our natural inclination is to seek something we desire, right? This is one reason why the pick-up paradigm is so seductive and sucks so many men in. So don't beat yourself up about falling into the pick-up trap. We'll talk later about steps to move away from this harmful work and hunting frame, and into a natural, loving co-creative Play-Frame. Before then, just start to be aware of the times when you get further and further into this kind of looped thinking, where you are deciding you need a result, then hunting it, therefore creating lack within yourself. When you drum in this story and live it again and again, you are allowing a deep wound of pain to resurface in yourself, and a story so convincing that you can't even remember any other way.

It's a story and pain, which you are creating by hunting. The pain you grow, however, feels very real indeed.

Let's examine this pain for a moment. Think right now about hunting. Imagine you are going out to do pick-up, to hunt. To acquire. Live into it for a moment. You need to get that which you somehow constantly lack and can never quite get. That elusive thing.

You see another hot girl walk past. You think about what the community would say in this moment. You know you should 'cold approach'. How does this feel in your body? Are you filled with appreciation for this lovely creature? Or do you now have a vague sense of ache or pain somewhere in your chest or throat, perhaps your heart space?

The pain of the hunter. Hunter's Anxiety is very real and has a physical representation. If you're feeling this pain, it's not because you're drinking too much coffee, it's because you are living life as a hunter and no one can hunt forever. You see this beautiful woman, like noticing a beautiful flower in the ground. Surely your body should fill with appreciation for her. But it doesn't, does it? You now feel pain and fear coursing through your body. This is the feeling the pick-up community creates and builds on. This is why it's so harmful.

Cure the Pain and Stop Trying to Comb the Mirror!

We'll go into this in great detail later on, but this pain and feeling of lack began a long time ago, when you were a child. All of us have experienced childhood trauma and abandonment which wounded our hearts, and which stays with us unless we begin a path towards healing.

Whatever the cause of your traumas of pain or sense of lack, it began a long time ago. The pain makes us begin feeling like we need to acquire something from outside of us to make the pain stop. So we start hunting and trying to acquire these things from an outside source.

When in pain, most people think they have to change the environment and the events around them to change that pain. They try to change things in the outside world, for instance—hunting women to get laid. They think pain is a result of the unfortunate circumstances in the outside world. In fact, the pain has always been there, and it was the pain that first started creating this story of lack.

We take that story of lack— "I'm not good enough, I'm unworthy to be loved", and this story is projected out into the world and then it is reflected back. More circumstances and events occur, reinforcing lack and unworthiness to be loved. Separation from women and what we desire begins as a knock-on effect, instead of enhancing the beautiful connection and opportunity that is already there.

Trying to change events to cure the pain is like trying to comb the mirror to do your hair. Stop trying to change events in the outside world. Stop hunting. Start addressing the pain directly within you. Heal your heart and the world changes correspondingly. You will become whole, fulfilled, full of natural expression, and that is the new story you will project onto the world.

And guess what... the world is going to reflect back some pretty amazing things.

Why the Hunter is Never Fulfilled

To some people the word 'hunter' sounds kinda cool. It's seen as the warrior that courageously moves towards its target. But you know what you really are if you're a pick-up hunter? You're a 'grasper'. You are desperately grasping for something, like a man dying of thirst, desperately crawling over burning sands towards a mirage and every time he reaches the hill where the mirage is, suddenly it's on the next hill and on he crawls...

You can never fulfil that particular desire because of the tension created by your lack, and your constant trying to crawl away from it. The story of lack creates the circumstances of lack. Not the other way around. You are connected to women already. The instant you decide to hunt her, and grasp and 'approach', you throw up a huge distance and barrier between the two of you. You create this strange 'lack tension'. Suddenly, instead of just flowing and merging in a natural, excited, playful way, you are separating yourself from her in your minds-eye, driven by pain and attempting to use her to alleviate it, using your Work-Frame strategy to get that result at any cost.

You are repelling that elusive thing. Like magnets, two positives repel each other. Desire creates a (+) charge, however the lack tension caused by grasping creates a (+) charge, too. So they repel each other, and you repel women as a result. Instead, stop grasping. Stop existing from lack. Deal with your pain, and begin to feel fulfilled, and then invite. Inviting (in our metaphor of magnets) creates an opposite (-) charge, and so inviting and desiring can work together in unison to be an attractive force.

When we are working from a painful childhood story creating this deep feeling of lack, we are projecting these painful mental loops, full of desperation and grasping. But when we work on the pain directly within ourselves, we stop the painful stories that follow suit. We simply express desire when we feel it, we invite lovingly and what we desire flows into our lives.

If you're hard into pick-up, trying to acquire to fill a hole, you're just like Wile E. Coyote trying to catch that roadrunner. You're never going to catch him because you are chasing a mirage. You want a result to end your painful story but it's like going to the cinema and scraping and howling at the movie screen rather than observing what's being projected or where it's being projected from.

You integrate the pain from within and your own personal movie projects correspondingly. That's how it works.

Academy Exercise

Think of that elusive thing you can't seem to acquire. Now from that place of lack, feel the corresponding feeling in your body (heart or gut and put a hand over it and feel into it).

What can you feel?

Now go back to the first bit of homework I set you. Does this feeling connect to that deep energetic wound from childhood, which is emanating a story of lack onto your world and shaping your experience?

UltimateDatingProgram.com

Chapter 9 – Goose Soup

We move onto the next leg of our tour—Budapest and I take the guys out to Szimpla, which is an iconic ruin bar full of holiday makers and easy going hostelers.

We're off the clock and Sacha says he's going to go back to the apartment for an early night.

I feel like I could do with one too but as I am walking out, I telegraph eye contact with a cute Scandinavian girl. She holds my eye contact, and without blinking I allow the contact to draw me in like a vacuum until I am two feet away from her. Still maintaining eye contact with her, I nudge her friend who is sat next to her and say to her;

"Your mate just gave me the come-fuck-me eyes".

Instead of reacting in disgust, they just giggle and smile and I now think; "holy fuck, I could be in here".

I push the envelope a bit further...

"You know I have a theory about girls that go out in 2's—they are either having a heart-to-heart or are out to get laid, and let's be honest, this aint no heart-to-heart..."

Again they just laugh and smile and now I am thinking about pushing this even further...

"How about we all go back to my apartment and have some fun". This time I say it in deadpan and matter-of-fact manner.

Amazingly, they don't argue or even scoff at the idea. It's on.

Annoyingly, just at this point, a student walks in. He thinks he's doing me a favour by talking to the friend. I turn to him and let him know I'm doing just fine and if he could kindly leave me to do my thing!

I return to the interaction and the friend is now being chatted up by some ripped dude in a tight grey T-shirt, who is a bit of a stud to be fair.

I look at the other girl, and whisper discretely;

"Do you want to come back to mine and have sex?"

At that moment, she looks me dead in the eye and holds my look to see if I'm full of shit.

You'll notice girls will do this just after you put yourself out there, such as directly inviting them back to yours. It's their way of seeing if you are congruous with your words or just a beta male who's borrowed a pair of bollocks for the night.

I hold the eye contact with her, for what feels like 5 seconds. If I break before she does, that's it, finished. She finally breaks eye contact and looks away with a little cheeky grin out the corner of her mouth.

"C'mon lets get out of here". I say.

As I do, I take her gently by the wrist and go to pull her off her stool.

In that moment, I'm fully expecting her to yank her arm back, at which point I would just seamlessly dissolve back into the new now, by making it part of a funny comedy sequence or something. But she comes straight off the stool in one flowing movement and walks out with me.

As we leave the bar, I suddenly push her up against the wall and kiss her passionately but pull her away as she is leaning in for those last few moments. "Save it tiger", I say cheekily.

We get to outside my apartment and I get a text from Sacha;

"Right, unless someone brings a hot girl back in the next 5 minutes, I'm taking the master bedroom".

In that exact moment, I buzz up to the apartment for him to let us in!

As we walk in, she can see Sacha, Steve and James squeezed into the living room on their depressing fold up single beds and sofa to sleep on.

Triumphantly, I stride into the master bedroom. It felt like a glorious win!

"Are we allowed to make noise" she says, being considerate for the others in the adjacent room.

"Make *as much* noise as you can!" I reply.

Disaster though, it seems I should have taken the advice of the student earlier who said to avoid the French restaurant opposite the apartment, as the goose soup I had is now wreaking havoc with me. I have terrible diarrhoea and have to keep running to the toilet every 10 minutes, to pebble-dash the bowl.

This becomes a comedy sketch and James starts filming me running in and out of the bathroom saying he will edit it to the Benny Hill theme music.

Every time I try and have sex, I can feel like I'm about to shit myself and am focussing so much on puckering my arsehole that I can't get hard.

I run back to the toilet, James slides me some diarrhoea tablets and I decide the best course of action is to double drop an emergency Viagra.

20 minutes later, my face is burning hot and my eyeballs feel like they're going to pop out.

And *still* nothing.

I keep going down on her in the hope it will finally kick in. My tongue is absolutely nackered, and by this point she's had enough of the preamble and wants to get going.

C'mon, c'mon you bastard! I say to myself, looking at my floppy member.

She's hot too. She's smoking. If we don't have sex I'm going to fucking throw myself out the window!

"Don't you find me attractive", she says, making things even worse.

"Excuse me". I go back to the bathroom and bosh another Viagra.

I go back out.

We try a 69 and maybe because my mind is now focussed on something else, miraculously my cock gets hard, but I have another bowel movement. I go soft again.

"Excuse me".

I go back to the toilet and 1... 2 more Viagra's.

By this point, just to clarify—I've had 4 Viagra's. I have a tongue the colour of a fucking Smurf and I feel like I'm about to explode.

I give it the ol' chopper in the palm and eventually head back out to the bedroom.

Finally, I'm rock solid and we have crazy athletic sex until the sun comes up.

Then all of a sudden, the walls of the cheap Budapest hotel room are caving in on me, moving in and out like an accordion.

I'm finding it hard to talk.

I'm blacking out.

Jesus, I think I'm having a stroke.

I manage to calm myself down enough to avoid calling an ambulance but with my head still throbbing, and every organ in my body feeling like it's about to internally combust, there is no way I can sleep. With wired, blood-shot eyes, I lay back staring at the ceiling trying not to die until the others get up. I'm praying I can somehow get the morning off coaching.

"If you are coaching in the morning you must have sex like a normal person not a Greek god!" James tells me.

Little did he know, the efforts I went to! I put my clothes on, say goodbye to her and head out to coach. God only knows how I got through the day without collapsing, and that evening, I take the guys out to a nightclub the other side of the river in Buda.

We get there and... oh fuck me, she's there too.

"That was amazing last night, can I come back to yours again".

NO.FUCKING.CHANCE!

I convince her to stay in contact and we meet up again for round 2, actually 3 years later in Budapest when I move there to live.

I somehow managed to get through the 10 day boot camp, surviving off crumbs of sleep. Often not getting home until 6am each night and then be so wired from coaching that I didn't fall asleep until 9am or 10am and then have to be up coaching for 11. And then do another full day's coaching until the wee hours.

We moved onto Split, Croatia and I met a wonderful local girl Violeta who I spent many days with. She was so cool, she would show us places to go, and help wing-woman the students on night's out. We had an intimate connection so genuine that I knew we'd be friends for years to come, and we are 10 years later.

I was getting the tag as being the high energy, night-time guy, that could get things flirty and sexual fast, but I was bummed out that my insights and perspective weren't getting embraced.

There was a reason why I was attracting these women, and not suffering from all the usual headaches. It wasn't because I had become an indestructible PUA Robotron. It was because I had found a way of interacting which was genuinely natural, which was effortless and fun and not based on seeking results. Yet the results were taking care of themselves.

I was able to start articulating what I was doing in a way that the students would understand. I personally mentored one guy, Steve, at night and spent a couple hours showing him the perfect attitude, whereby I'm always playing and never in a state of judgment, or keeping score of my results, but just becoming the chaos. Being in a continuous flow. The penny drops for him too and he starts coasting round the bar chatting to every girl with total freedom...

"Damn! John, I *get* it now! It's like the girls are just a bonus to what you're already doing! It's like you're having fun, you notice girls around you, and you sweep them into what you're doing. If they don't want to, we haven't lost anything, we're not rejected. It's their loss if anything! We just carry on doing what we were already doing!"

Steve was having his first taste of my philosophy and adopting the core principles of Autonomy, Giving and Play.

The next day—Steve, whilst being coached by Sacha, gets told to 'cold approach' some 'sets' on the street. *Instantly*, it was like regressing back to the old way of doing things for Steve. Like going from a super computer with a parallel processor back to an 8-bit Commodore 64, suddenly he was now back in the PUA paradigm where he was being judged on his ability to achieve 'results' with girls.

He had had a taste of freedom but was suddenly back in the hunting mindset of PUA all over again. With that, he rips off the microphone he had under his shirt, which was being used by Sacha to listen into his interactions, and he storms off.

"Once you learn your way John, you can't go back", Steve states.

I was starting to think to myself; Hey, what I'm doing here and teaching isn't even Natural Game, as the Natural Gamers would all still be on the street hunting, still 'approaching', still trying to avoid 'rejection'. They were trying to control interactions all the way up to

65

the 'close'. What I'm teaching here, transcends that. But then how could it? Surely, it's just the same thing. Surely, it's just a very natural version of Natural Game. It irked me for a while. I knew deep down this was profoundly different—but I couldn't quite define it. I couldn't quite model out the difference, in a way that truly separated it.

Whenever I tried applying the PUA concepts like 'approach' and 'close' and 'rejection', whilst trying to explain what I was doing, it was like the slit experiment in quantum physics, where the power of observation collapses the wave function. Similarly, the simple use of these concepts snapped me and my students back into the Work-Frame PUA paradigm again. Suddenly, we were now having to blast through anxiety all over again.

I needed a way to embody this so that everyone could see and feel the difference.

Academy Exercise

When you go out at night, instead of the scoring system being geared around your results with women, on the stroke of each hour, you will give yourself a score out of 10 how much fun you are having. What was your highest number and total number?

UltimateDatingProgram.com

Chapter 10 – From Pick-up Artist to Social Heartist

Textbook pick-up artistry

I went back to the UK and I started coaching guys in London. I don't know what it was, maybe being back in a big city, maybe being back surrounded by entitled English girl brats again but by the time I went on the next European tour a few months later, I felt a bit flat.

It's strange but as much as I had distanced myself from the PUA mindset and this need to acquire—I was feeling a pressure to bonk girls and keep my rep up in front of the pick-up coaches and students, to not look like a fraud. It was all ego-based nonsense but as the tour went on, I felt an urgency to constantly prove myself, and as a result I noticed my behaviour slip back into acquisition.

Despite a couple of hook ups en route, I was becoming more and more frantic and by the time we're in Belgrade, Serbia (which was a new addition to the tour), my sense of play and freedom had gone. I'm seeing the social territory like a PUA again...

I'm walking along the beach by the lake. I 'approach', 'open' and 'lock in' with a '2-set' who are sitting on the sand.

I secretly like one of the girls but don't let it show straight away. I befriend them both, especially 'disarming' the friend, and position myself closest to the one I like... 'the target'.

As I go to 'number close', I hand the phone to my 'target', so as to appear serendipitous.

Later that evening I ring her and invite her out...

"Meet someone I've only just met—*really?*" she says.

"Yeah you're right, can I trust you?" I say, cleverly reversing the psychology on her.

"Haha ok, very clever, I'll meet you".

We meet by the horse statue in Belgrade and because the context had been friends up to now, as she arrives I 'kino' her and spin her round and say "WOW, you look sexy", 'pre-framing' the meeting as something more romantic.

I have the map already planned out. I am staying in an apartment close to the student park, so I take her for a drink in a bar right outside the apartment. In the conversation I am carefully taking note of key signposts in what she is saying. She mentioned her love for photography and how she is doing a photo shoot soon. I take the opportunity to put myself forward as a model.

"We can start today, lets go up to my place and I'll put something nice on, and you can take pictures of the city from the amazing view".

Hesitantly, she agrees as I 'bounce' her up to my apartment. As we are taking the long walk up into the apartment, I use a bit of misdirection to take her mind off the awkward pressure building up, during the walk, to prevent a 'state break'.

"Hey, what do you think of my photography?"

I quickly show her the pictures on my phone.

When she arrives in the apartment, I go into my bedroom and she takes pictures of the view outside. I wait in my bedroom for her. As she eventually comes in, I start kissing and undressing her and we have sex.

Later that evening just as she is leaving, the rest of the boys are coming back to the apartment. As she leaves, they high five me and tell me what a great pick-up that was.

That girl never spoke to me again.

The Way of The Social Heartist

The encounter bothered me. I should have been stoked that I got with this hot girl, but I felt lousy about it. I wasn't even sure *why* exactly at this point. I go back to coaching the students on the street. The sun is shining, I'm on an adventure, I'm with my friends and life is good, I remind myself.

On the streets of Belgrade you get stopped a lot by beggars, gypsies, kids, and bizarre street sellers. If you give money, you get tapped on the head and blessed. If you don't, you get a curse muttered at you. I'm feeling good so I decide to give 200 dinars to one of the legit street charity workers, working for animal cruelty. In return, I get given a card with two cute puppies cuddling on it.

Walking around holding it, what would normally happen is, it ends up on the mantelpiece or in the bin eventually. But perhaps because I was feeling so good, I felt inspired to do something creative, so I use the opportunity to write a soppy message on the inside...

Hey...You must be pretty damn special if you got this, so smile and let your inner beauty shine!

Much like the feeling of sending an anonymous message in a bottle, into the ocean—I couldn't wait to give it to someone, knowing the magic it would create.

Jon, who I am with, asks who I will give it to. "I am not sure yet", I tell him. I will wait until it *just feels right*.

As I walk around, instead of focusing on 'approaching' hot girl 'targets', I open up the range of possibility to everyone. Perhaps someone sad, perhaps a child busker, perhaps the humour of giving it to a big, muscled dude!

The intention was all-encompassing and as a result it was like my heart started opening. By this point, the card in my hand became the physical expression of my internal state and my intention. The card and myself at this point are one and the same. I am glowing with a feeling of aliveness and this creative sparkle.

From this point, my only possible role is one of giving away this gift to someone. As I'm walking around, I know that I have the creative potential to offer a poetic gesture, something unique and touching for anyone that passes me by. I know that it is worthy of making someone's day if I simply walk over and give it to them. I focus on that feeling.

I had reached a point of no expectation of reciprocity, and that's unconditional. I had cleared my motives, fostered a karmic attitude of c'est la vie, and instead of looking to pick-up and acquire specific objects and targets—the environment became a big pool of potential and possibility.

I was offering out from this abundant source of overflow—like an infinite fountain that replenishes instantly. I knew I was about to do something amazing, and my body glittered in anticipation. I had focused my intention on that and because I was 100% outward orientated, I had removed all concerns of trying to keep myself safe. Anxiety couldn't exist in this state. It had transmuted and I was now in the field of my heart. Integrated with my surroundings.

As I walk around, I am looking into the eyes and faces of the passers-by, with the anticipation to give to them if I so wished. But there was no pressure to. I feel connected to everyone, because I am holding onto the intention to want to create with any and all of them.

Not only that, but I feel like I'm noticing it affect the people around me. It's like the vibes coming off me are drawing people into my orbit. People are starting to notice me more.

I feel powerful as I walk around, but not from a place of manipulation and control, but from a place of total freedom that comes from a willingness to create.

We stop on the main drag, with people circled around a violinist. I look across and in that moment my eyes meet a girl's. Nothing needs to be said. My eyes have become little windows to my internal sunshine feeling, and as we make eye-contact she looks at me and feels it. She looks away quickly, then looks back. Our eyes meet again, followed by a smile. I glide round and without any strategy or prepared lines, and without any 'approaching', I introduce myself.

Instead of giving her the card in my hand, I give her the gift of the feeling I had and my masculine presence. I don't need to verbalise it because it is felt.

By presenting myself in this way, there is an immediate resonance that would not have been possible if I was 'running Game' or trying to covertly hoodwink her with a mentally rehearsed strategy. She feels this vibe. Everything flows. It feels effortless. Simple.

Me: "Hi, who are you?"

"Fine, thank you".

"Ha, I meant *who* are you?"

"Haha, Ivana".

"Hi Ivana, I'm John, shall we... go for a walk?"

I invite her and her friend to join us for a drink and as we are walking down the street together, it feels 'just right' and I pass her the card.

She goes silent for a minute and then wipes away a tear.

We spend the rest of the trip together and have an insane connection on all levels. She later confesses the encounter including the card were the most beautiful things she had ever experienced. Because it was unique and from the heart and that's rare. Oh, and almost a decade later, she is the one of the most special girls in my life and we talk regularly even though she lives in the USA.

Now, can you see the difference in those two stories?

The first example was coming from control and strategy and coming from that place of needing to get a result to feel complete. I was a taker.

The second example was total freedom, as I felt content—expressing from a place of joy and play. I was a creator.

It was an epiphany. Although only fleetingly, I had lived and breathed what it was like to be *completely* natural.

I then returned to the Natural Gamers all hunting on the street:

"Go and 'cold approach' that set".

"Ah man, I'm getting 'approach anxiety', I should blast through it".

"What do I 'open' with when I 'lock in'?"

WTF! It was like unplugging from the PUA matrix and looking in. The command & conquer actions now seemed ugly and jarring. It was a big awakening. Natural Game as much as it was dressed up, was still bloody Game! It was just another tent in the same circus.

For a bit I thought I had woken up to a healthy, more evolved way of interacting with women, but like the movie Inception, I had just woken up into another dream.

Walking around the streets of Belgrade, I had moved beyond judgments, limitations, constructs, winning or losing, strategies and control. I was broadcasting a whole new vibe out into the world. There was no approaching, no rejection, no anxiety. Instead of predicting the worst-case scenarios and battling with self-inflicted hunter's anxiety, I was trusting in the unknown, and exploring the potential and possibility, from a place of freedom and pure creation, with the same child-like sense of adventure and wonder as a child running into a playground on a warm summer's day. It was ecstatic.

It was at this point I knew I hadn't just discovered the latest evolution of Game. This was beyond Game. This was *Game Over*.

It was quite a unique and profound experience, however I started to reflect back on all those moments where everything had clicked so effortlessly with girls in the past—and realised it was because, just like this experience, I was navigated by the heart. Like the heart of a child that just wants to play and create with people, without any agenda or need for an outcome. A state of fearlessness through *unconditionality*.

Whereas all the times where I had lost my mojo and things felt like so much hard work, was because I was projecting from my broken-heart and my lack-tension and had slipped into control-mode. I was then trying to defy anxiety and battle it head on, blast through it, destroy it!

I had 20-20 vision. Natural Game (like all forms of Game) was all about scarcity and taking. This was about abundance and **Giving**. Natural Game was about working *for* outcomes. This was about **Playing** *with* women. Natural Game was about expectation and hesitation, this was about **Autonomy**, spontaneity and creation.

One was fear, the other love.

One was Pick-up artistry, this was **Social Heartistry.**

Social Heartistry Meditation

To experience a bit of that magic I felt walking around the streets of Belgrade—as a visualisation, imagine back when you were a kid, and it's a hot summer's day, and you can't wait to get outside and have fun. There's a water slide and a paddling pool in the garden. Excitedly, you run and climb to the top.

As you do, I want you to climb your awareness up to your eyeballs and as you go down the slide, drop your awareness quickly from your eyes into your heart space, as if it's gone down the slide. As you hit the water, imagine a big *SPLASH* with the water cascading outwards, and outwards and outwards. Connect to that feeling.

Do you notice a feeling of dropping in and expanding outwards simultaneously from the heart space?

Then, as the excited kid, you want to do it again, and again! So, you go climb back up the steps and drop back down into the water, and again, this wave of sheer joy rippling out from you.

Academy Exercise

Create your own unconditional gift, for instance a little note scribbled on a bit of paper, a rose made from a paper napkin. Whatever the idea, try and make it unique from you, and then spend an hour walking around, with the intention to give it to a random stranger. Allow yourself to be open to give it to anyone. Tune into the feeling of knowing this could make someone's day. How do you feel in your body doing this? Do concepts like 'approach' and rejection' exist for you in this state?

UltimateDatingProgram.com

75

Chapter 11 – Hole-Hearted or Wholehearted?

I had now *finally* made sense of my journey. I realise how I went from being natural around women, to then getting derailed, feeling hopeless, then getting enticed into PUA Pleasure Island, where I then became a jackass.

The pick-up industry had drawn me in because I was broken-hearted and deep in pain from my break up. I was egged on by the industry, to make up for it; ANY girl, ANY time, ANY place! Pretty good substitute, right?

I found pick-up and acquisition so alluring because my heart had closed, so I was operating from my pain and lack. With a closed-heart, I looked outside myself to acquire girls to mask over the top of it and acquire affection, to prove to myself that I was accepted.

It's a kind of mixture of fear, pain, and fear of that pain, that I had been holding onto for so long, that I didn't even consciously realise it at the time, but it was driving my actions.

So, let's take a look at what this pain and lack really is—and where it originated.

Childhood Coping Mechanisms

When you were a child, your heart was whole. You beamed love onto the world around you. I can say that with confidence because almost every child begins like that. But your heart was so wide open that you eventually got hurt. You suffered a trauma—a trauma of abandonment and feelings of unworthiness to be loved. I can also say this with confidence because everyone experiences it. It's all subjective. For some of us it was a parent actually dying or leaving, and for others it was a smaller thing like feeling temporarily unwanted.

For me, the trauma was thinking my parents didn't love me as much as my sister. I then went about trying to rationalise why I wasn't equally loved. The mind of a little child is not a very logical place and at that age we can experience a great trauma from events that as adults we might say was a bit silly. To our 4 or 5 year old minds it's very serious indeed. That sense of abandonment feels like we are dying inside. Like a hole is being torn in our hearts.

As children we are very intuitively clever and because we don't want to sit in our nervous system and feel this pain—which if you can imagine feeling for the first time, must have been hell—we learn various ways to avoid or pacify it. We may suck on our dummies, sleep through it or cry for attention. We may try to control and acquire pleasure as a coping mechanism, to superimpose a more pleasant sensation over the top of the pain. We may also try and avoid the pain by intellectualising it—going into our heads and creating a story about ourselves that we are useless and probably undeserving of being loved.

As we continue to find ways to avoid or pacify that pain, over time, that wound and corresponding story gets pushed under the carpet but stays with us, becoming a deep part of our minds and personalities.

77

As we move into adolescence, we are red-raw with testosterone and more often than not our sexual energy is not fulfilled. We often masturbate as a way to pacify the frustrating lack tension this creates.

We start to make habits of these pacification methods that fill emptiness, take away loneliness, get attention or avoid pain. It becomes a 'filling of the hole' you could say—an addiction, using external gratification as a way to avoid taking responsibility for the actual feeling, much like a heroin user needs a hit to feel balanced.

In adulthood, we still fight hard to keep ourselves filled. If you haven't spent any time working on that core trauma, then you still have this deep pain caused by a hole torn in your heart. It's there lurking beneath everything you are and everything you do.

Filling the Void to Avoid the Feeling

Later in life, even if we start to feel fine, another traumatic event (especially some sort of abandonment event) can tear that hole wide open again and it's one of the most painful things we can ever experience. It certainly was for me after losing my girlfriend at the time.

After much self-exploration work, I now realise, it wasn't the break up that created the empty, broken-hearted feeling. It was the same wound first created in childhood that was opened once more. A wound that had resurfaced. By this point, I would do *anything* to avoid that pain. I believed I needed to chase things around me to cure that wound, to fill that hole. What did I decide to use to fill it with? Hunting girls! I invented this crazy rule (like most guys in that situation) that if I could just get a girl naked with me then the pain would go away. Sound familiar?

Hole-Hearted, the Pick-up Way

When you live with this wound and you hunt women to make it go away, you become desperate and needy. You really do need to acquire and achieve that result, or you feel like the pain will get worse and your ego thinks it might die. You are now in *survival* mode. Coming from a place of ego-survival, you naturally give off a needy smell. Girls can smell it a mile off and it repels them...

You are moving through life with an agenda. You are so desperate you can't even relax and have fun anymore—your emotional well-being is now on the line. You have pain creating this lack and creating the sort of behaviour that would make Pac-Man blush. You need a result. You need that damn result!

The PUA Shield

Now, because we know neediness is unattractive to women, especially high self-esteem women, instead of addressing and integrating that pain and moving to a place of Autonomy and freedom, the community adopt the surface-level counteracting techniques & behaviours to batten down the hatches and disguise this needy smell. These compensatory techniques include;

Acting like the Alpha-Male, being Cocky-Funny, Qualifying her, Disqualifying yourself, showing Active Disinterest, 'Negging', False-Time Constraints (pretending you only have a limited amount of time), leaving kisses off texts, leaving X amountof days to call her back.

I could go on all day about the different tactics the community comes up with to hide the needy smell.

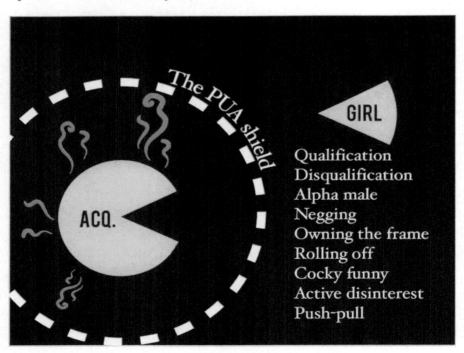

Yet here's the paradox, they are all simply masks. All of them simply techniques to give the illusion you are a non-needy, autonomous guy, all the while really neeeeding this woman!

This is what's known as *behavioural dissonance*. You are trapped in the pick-up paradigm, desperate for an outcome to get your fix. The more you think this way, the 'better' you rattle off your pick-up performance, but the needier you become and the more you repel women. As this needy smell grows and grows, you try to hide it with all sorts of PUA shield techniques so you appear non-needy. You're trying to drown the smell in cheap aftershave and this behavioural dissonance is what women refer to as 'creepy'.

You may have started off desiring women from appreciation and wanting to be intimate with them, but now that you have actively involved yourself in PUA Pleasure Island, you have amplified that neediness—that lack.

Other pick-up dudes, all comparing themselves and competing with each, other now surround you. Holding the bragging rights over whether they were more successful or not.

You ask yourself— "am I a PUA or a loser?"

The moment you begin to question yourself in this way, your self-esteem plummets as your sense of personal value is now directly linked to your ability to reap results or not.

It's a slippery slope. Has it happened to you?

Perhaps you remember starting from a strong place of purpose and autonomy in your life but deteriorated and fell into this trap?

This was how it occurred for me, if you remember?

Wholehearted, the Social Heartistry Way

Someone who's got a hole in the heart needs to take and someone who's wholehearted can give, endlessly—like the sun.

Now, imagine for a moment you don't have this gaping wound in you. You don't desperately need an outcome. You've carefully worked to heal and integrate yourself.

You are healthy, content and spilling this out into the world like an infinite fountain from a deep groundswell of creative potential. Your heart is whole. Doesn't that sound fricking awesome? *That,* my friend is the Social Heartistry way.

When you integrate your pain and enjoy being comfortable in your own skin, you don't need to try and hide anything, or use tricks. You are able to let go and just PLAY. You are free from outcomes and agendas. You are free from conflicts, free from pain, free from fear of loss and as a result, *extremely* attractive.

Pick-Up	Social Heartistry
Taking	**Giving**
Working	**Playing**
Neediness	**Autonomy**
Conditional	Unconditional
Win/Lose	Win/Win
Filling a Hole	Feeling Whole
Manipulating	Creating
Mental Masturbation	Instinct & Intuition
Seeking Outcomes	Exploring Potential
Hesitation	Spontaneity
Childish	Child-like
Limitation	Limitless
Approaching	Attracting
Gaming	Living
Surviving	Thriving
FEAR	LOVE

Academy Exercise

A good habit of getting into a giving mindset rather than one of taking, is to carry out 10 random acts of kindness to strangers. Be creative. It could be as small as a compliment, or as big as taking a homeless person for a coffee. It is done because you *want* to do it, from a place of giving unconditionally, not hoping to get something back. It is also not just performed on the first beautiful girl you see. That would be missing the point, right?

UltimateDatingProgram.com

Chapter 12 – Healing the Heart

As you start to heal your heart, you too will move from being a pick-up artist to becoming the Social Artist. The two things together in unison—the inner healing and the outer expression, from heart-centred awareness, is what I refer to as **Social Heartistry.**

You will notice yourself pulling away from the PUA community. You will watch less and less videos, attend fewer bootcamps, read less PUA theory, and drop your wingmen. You will return to balance and harmony, and return to being a healthily integrated man again. Maintaining his desire and impact with people and the world around you.

Right now, you may be enjoying talking to more women than ever before, and by all means this type of action is great—never lose that. However, now you know you can talk to just as many women, but without having to go on the hunt for them. Without going through all the cocaine highs and lows of this addictive and toxic Acquisition-based Work-Frame.

Awareness

The first stage is awareness. To have awareness that you may be guarding a deep pain and your hunting actions within Game are a reaction to that pain. If you are unprepared to be humble and open to this—have an inclination to defend Game to the hills, there is very little that will change.

For instance, you may shriek "but pick-up works".

Well, I could say begging works. In fact, I once got stopped in Victoria station by a guy in a smart suit. He told me he was on his way to court and needed exactly £2.50 to get a train ticket. I gave it to him. The next month, I was in another part of town, and got stopped by the same guy in a suit, telling me he needed £2.50 to go to court! When I told him I saw him before, he scuttled off embarrassed.

Now you could say what he's doing 'works'. He's spending his days sneakily extracting money from people. He's probably a rich boy! But in my mind, he is not winning at life. He is very poor in my eyes. So even if you say pick-up works: "I went out and did pick-up and it worked", you may think you have scored, but really you have successfully begged—filled your hole for a fleeting moment—but your emptiness and pain prevails ultimately.

Imagine the heroin addict who is desperate for his hit to feel balanced. He is then presented with two different coaches:

1. Hey man, if you work with me, I can make sure you get your hit by the end of the weekend. Not only that but you'll never run out of heroin *ever* again

2. Hey man if you work with me, you'll never *need* heroin, and be dependent on it and you can lead a balanced and harmonious life

Which one do you think most addicts would choose in that moment?

One is the quick fix; the band-aid solution that does not last forever and the second example is the real work, the real success.

Do you want to be a guy that's in constant hunt mode, hunting every cute girl you see, trying desperately to stockpile girls, driven by never-ending anxiety and emptiness, or do you want to feel balanced and harmonious, even without girls?

This is a critical question to ask yourself.

Acceptance: Loving Mother Work

The next stage is where we reconnect to ourselves and do the healing work. This is our effort to reconnect to the parts of us that we have neglected for all our adult lives. Eckhart Tolle would call it the pain body. Jung would call it the shadow. I refer to this healing work as Loving Mother work, but it could also be called loving acceptance work, inner child work or inner bonding work.

Can you feel into that feeling of lack right now? Visualise that elusive thing you can't get fulfilment from (say girls) and feel how you can't quite reach it. Feel that grasping, that lack tension. Go deep into that feeling and you'll experience a pain, an energetic blockage in your heart space, gut, or perhaps somewhere else. Sometimes it feels like a dull ache, a cold/hot sensation, a feeling of sorrow, loneliness or as one of my students says; "like battery acid pouring in the heart".

Sometimes it comes on at the most irrational of times, other times we get provoked in certain situations.

For instance, I was once having a drink with a girl I was dating, and after a couple drinks she said she had to go to see a friend and I later saw her with a guy on a date.

Now, they could have been just friends, but my little child reacted, and I could feel this ache in my heart. The story that accompanied it was "I am unworthy to be loved", "I'm not good enough". From that feeling of unworthiness I wanted to get away from it. I went and knocked back a couple pints and that numbed me out for the evening.

Has something like this ever happened to you? I know it's happened to most guys. So replay the incident within your mind, and imagine those painful feelings exactly as you experienced it originally.

Instead of feeling unworthiness in this way and reacting by reaching out for stimulations and tranquilisers such as porn, movies, cigarettes, alcohol, drugs (or doing pick-up). Instead, feel into the fire and sit with the feeling. It's hard at the start, I know! But this is what needs our attention. This is when we start the healing. We have to go through it, just as we accept a looming cold winter.

However, in society we are encouraged to chase happiness... Chase the dopamine highs and suppress the lows. This is in effect, seeking the light and avoiding the shadow—the pain. This is how our culture works. It feeds off the collective pain body and its propensity to move towards avoidance of the shadow/pain.

It's no different with the culture of pick-up. But it's a double-edged sword, because as we champion the acquisition of pleasures (the perceived light) we are conversely condemning our pain (the shadow), and we are creating an imbalance. So now we're in inner conflict between the lower and higher parts within ourselves and because we are inwardly divided, we therefore view the world outwardly as separated and divided. The intention and language of pick-up then reinforces the division, both inwards and outwards, which I explain in depth later on.

We must learn to embrace the pain, the darkness, and integrate it to reach a place of inner balance. To not do this kind of work is like the sword saying, "Nah, I don't want to go through the blacksmith's fire". If that's so, then you're not a real sword, are you?

When we do this autonomous cleansing of our psyches, our worldview changes correspondingly and we can lead a more healthy life coming from our highest potential. When we're not integrating our pain, we are being abusive to ourselves, and this can lead to corresponding abusive actions to others. That is why you see pick-up coaches take on sociopathic behaviour, such as using women as collateral damage for more YouTube views. Leading her on camera, all the way to the bedroom, then as this woman believes she had a genuine connection, is now on YouTube for the world to see.

Anyone who abuses others for the sake of further advancement are the most in pain, and in my experience, the people *most* in pain are the PUA coaches. That's why we have the common expression: the doctors are often more in pain than the patients. In fact, the very first page of The Game by Neil Strauss, Mystery-the-so-called guru is having a mental breakdown.

Alchemy: Inner Bonding Meditation

So let's begin. Start off by sitting upright on your bed cross-legged, you can sit with your back to the backboard. Now tune into the 'lack tension'and any abandonment/unworthiness feeling. You may not feel anything. That's ok. We have suppressed this part of ourselves for so long that it's often buried deep within.

Bring your attention to your nostrils and feel the cold air coming in and the warm air gong out. Keep your awareness here for a minute or so, then as you exhale, let the air completely release until there is that void space where you neither inhale nor exhale. Now hold onto this no-breath period, and simultaneously drop and sink your awareness down into your chest/heart space.

In the silence, tune in with any feelings there. Then as you tune in, you can start breathing again whilst maintaining awareness on that area.

The feelings may be subtle and bland or acute and seemingly painful, but tune in to it regardless, and keep your awareness there.

For the next five minutes, just feel the feeling. If your mind wanders, that's okay—don't judge it. Just seamlessly bring it back to the feeling. Track that feeling, see if it changes in intensity or moves to other areas of the body. Cradle this feeling like a mum would cradle her child that is upset.

Little You

If you're having trouble tuning into the feeling, as a visualisation, imagine walking into your bedroom when you were a kid and seeing yourself. And I want you, as the loving parent, ask the little you; "Are you ok? What do you need?"

Do not force yourself onto the 'little you' but be humble instead. Perhaps you imagine knocking on the door to the bedroom and asking humbly if it's ok to come in and connect. Deep in that state of feeling what you feel, allow the answers to arise. If you do not have anything come up, that's fine. Just return back to experiencing the feeling and tracking it. Be the calm empathic rock for that child.

That means not allowing yourself to be drawn into the wound but rather be the larger transformative source, like the calm loving adult who sees the pain of the child but remains strong and loving. This is empathy and is different to sympathy. Sympathy by definition is putting yourself emotionally into another person's shoes. And this means sharing a wound vibrationally. Empathy in this sense is acknowledging someone else's pain yet not being part of that pain.

We are able to channel a higher transformative source to heal and give support to the child. This is what we mean when we say 'self-love' and is why I've called it Loving Mother work. It's the internalising, the nurturing, the feminine side of us.

Now, as you finish, take 3 deep breaths in and whilst you do it, smile. Breathe into the smile and let that smiling breath refresh your inner child.

To start with, I recommend you do this when you wake up and before you go to sleep. Of course, we can't be perfect so don't worry if you can't do it *every* day. But aim to do it regularly, to gradually reconnect with yourself and your inner child and begin healing. And certainly, do it when you get provoked or feel like you are reacting, pacifying or avoiding.

Change: Loving Father Work

After reconnecting with our little inner child through Loving Mother work, there comes a time when we have to step back out into the busy world. At this point we have to be the loving father who goes out and fends for himself and his child. This is what I call *Loving Father work.*

So, after building up this trust and reconnecting to the little us, we have to then say to our child-self that we must now go out into the world. Just like in reality when we are comforting a child who is upset, at some point the adult must leave the child and return to his work or responsibilities. Too much of the Loving Mother work and no real action in the world is no good to us.

Loving Father work is us interfacing and creating with the world. It's the *action* taking, the externalising, the masculine side of us. It's us penetrating the world. We are a man of purpose on a trajectory.

This is another way we heal—through purpose. This could be our careers, our side-hustles, or even just a small hobby or passion that excites us and we can envisage it building. In its truest form, loving father work is the moment we wake up and realise what our core gifts are, and we bring this to the world from a place of service. Even if you do not have this larger purpose in full vision, the intention is that you are moving towards whatever you're working on in your daily life and constantly growing.

Become Yourself

You'll often hear people say, "just be yourself". Being yourself is only half the story. 'Being' is solely the feminine aspect, which maintains and accepts the current state of affairs. We can sit in our mum's basement playing Xbox all our lives, but I'm pretty sure that's not what the universe intended for us. Do you actually believe you have manifested the fullness of your potential and capacity yet? If not, that means you're still coming, you're still arriving.

Therefore, we should not just BE ourselves. That is just sitting in our feminine acceptance energy. As my mentor Darren Deojee says, you BE/COME yourself (Being + Coming). It is the integration of the masculine energy of *coming,* which is responsible for change and growth, whilst also *accepting* ourselves and any eventuality along the way, with grace.

Everyday with your intention on you BE/COMING, you emanate this. As you walk around, you are the embodiment of a man who is constantly growing, on his path of becoming.

Now, when we see women we find attractive, we interact with them grounded in our dynamically growing and evolving soul on our own unique journey.

91

We only have to open our mouth and it emanates out. It seeps out through every pore in our body. She can feel it. This alignment with purpose is our wholeness, and anything that happens with women is insignificant to this larger calling. We are autonomous.

Imagine in *The Wizard of Oz* and their journey to the Emerald City. If they fall off the path, they will always remember their path and return to it. Most people who get into pick-up or are hunting girls for happiness don't have a path, and so they gravitate towards the distractions and the superficial highs—the avoidance mechanisms, the filling of the hole, and so forth.

We expect women to fill our emptiness but it's a trap. Don't look for women to complete you. Instead of meeting women as fragmented beings, meet as two whole beings. That way you come together with women from a place of inter-dependence, sharing, creating, as opposed to co-dependence, acquisition and manipulating. Even in a relationship, don't look your partner in the eyes. Stand next to each other and look in the same direction.

This is real autonomy and is the first Social Heartistry principle…

Academy Exercise

Write a letter to yourself from 10 years in the future. Write down what you are doing and carefully describe every detail. How do you feel knowing you have accomplished all the things you wanted to do? Tune into that feeling. By having that vision and through the law of resonance, you can start manifesting your dream reality, day by day.

UltimateDatingProgram.com

Chapter 13 – Principle #1: Autonomy

Ultimately, the process of moving from being a pick-up hunter to an attractive creator starts from deep within and integrating our pain, and learning to be more comfortable in our own skin, but what does this look like in the social world? How do we express ourselves in a way which doesn't fall back into the hunting mindset?

Firstly, by simply dropping judgment. In this way we don't set ourselves up for the fall because there's no judgment around our interactions with women anymore. There's no longer judgment at every moment—where we worry if one interaction or another is successfully moving towards the outcome we desperately need.

"So what? I don't talk to girls now John? I don't try and get laid? Shall we all become a bunch of monks?" **Facebook comment**

Now this is imperative so listen up—transcending judgment does not mean transcending human contact. It does not mean avoiding women, sitting at the side of the bar saying "Hey, I don't have to talk to any girls now!"

That's just keeping yourself safe. That just means you've disconnected and are still filling your ego with safety by not allowing yourself to be exposed.

Transcending judgment is about moving from the perceived need for an outcome, to complete detachment from an outcome.

Personally, I don't like the word 'detachment'. It sounds like giving up or disconnecting. Giving up is conceding defeat to that which we previously desired. We then continue to resonate with that something and feel the despair of not attaining it.

We're still in a Work-Frame— we've just given up on the outcome, which we still crave.

The Essence of Autonomy

Instead of 'detachment', I prefer to use the word Autonomy—which is one of my 3 core Social Heartistry principles. It reframes detachment and puts it into the affirmative action, giving us something tangible to hang our hat on, rather than just 'detaching'. Detaching into what exactly?

No, my friend. You are going to find Autonomy, like the sun.

Autonomy is shifting our focus and fulfilment from seeking specific results with women (pick-up) to enjoying what we're already doing in that moment. Whether it's enjoying our friends, the music, the sunshine, going to the gym, dancing—going anywhere on our way with purpose, or just being fulfilled in our own presence without seemingly doing anything.

When we return to this state, we spill this fulfilment outwards to the people around us including girls we like. Being detached/ autonomous in this sense is letting go of the need for an outcome and allowing what is, whilst still participating *fully* and bringing all our masculine desire and action to bare. Yeah, you can actually do both! And a true 'natural' does—not a natural gamer, a natural person.

Set the intention, take action and…. LET GOOOO

Letting go means every moment and every eventuality is accepted because there's no judgment, no measurement, no win or lose, no need to control an outcome. In this place of no judgment (equanimity) is where all the fun stuff happens.

By removing judgment, it turns limitation and suffering into possibility and potential, because when every moment is accepted and embraced there is no need to force anything. Everything is just dandy.

Observe a piece of music being played. Certain high notes are being hit and certain low notes are also hit. But there is no judgment whether high or low. We don't sulk when a low note is hit and get excited when a high note is hit. We transcend the judgment on the ups and down because we are focused on the music. The music embraces all notes equanimously because it's in a continuous *flow*.

Similarly, the Social Artist focuses on his music—his expression and the way he interacts with people. Sometimes people will respond well, some not. But within his music he keeps playing devotedly.

Be the Pinball, My Friend

I often teach my students the metaphor of a pinball. When it is fired off it has a kinetic motion—a momentum of its own, and it moves towards parts of the table and pings around, then all of a sudden it goes into the main feature and the table lights up and a huge rack of points go on the board. Then the ball comes out and bounces off other parts and then perhaps ends up in the gulley to be fired again. At any point though, when the ball bounces off something, or narrowly misses out on entering into the main feature, does it lose momentum? It doesn't see that as a 'rejection' or loss.

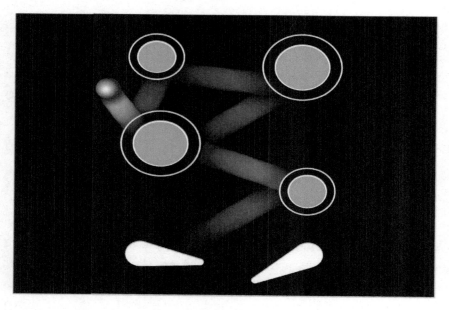

The pinball has transcended the win or lose Work-Frame on everything it comes into contact with. It moves without judgment. It does not fixate or judge one thing over another. It does not lose momentum, only gains it. It is fluid, it's free, and it's in a continuous *flow*.

The Barman Attitude

When I worked as a barman I would flirt outrageously with girls over the bar. Kiss them, ask for their number, set up meetings later after work—yet at no point as I was talking to them over the bar, was it an 'approach'. I was just serving them drinks, and the flirting was absorbed into this higher purpose of just being a barman. If they didn't play along, I pass them the drink and without any judgment, move on to serve the next customer in one seamless action. Notice how I say 'move on to', not 'approach'. At no point is it a 'rejection' or a 'blow out', either. A barman is never 'rejected' is he? That paradigm doesn't exist. A barman never 'approaches', despite the fact he talks and flirts with 100's of girls he sees during the night. This is because he has Autonomy, he has a higher purpose to serve drinks and he'll always fall back into that action. Because of this context, he has transcended Acquisition and the win or lose Work-Frame and ultimately transcended pick-up. He is free.

The Musician on Stage

Imagine you're at Wembley Arena, and on stage is Axl Rose and he's belting out "Sweet Child of Miiiiiinnnnee" to 100,000 people. As he's trotting around on stage, totally in his element, he puts his hand down into the crowd to where he sees a hot girl. She doesn't touch his hand. Is Axl 'rejected?' Through the pick-up goggles he is, but someone that is always in their Autonomy is never rejected, as they go back to what they were *already* doing. Go and watch any musician play live. When they perform, they are not there to take your approval, or convert you to their music. Their intention is to provide their music as an offering. They are not begging for anything, and not looking to acquire anything from the listener. They are expressing themselves through the music. It is an outward-orientated intention. In the true sense they are artists.

As I interact with a woman, in the same spirit, I am the artist, not with a piano or violin but with my attitude and expression. I am presenting an opportunity, I am playing my music, I am inviting her to step into my orchestra and play her music with me. If we don't harmonise, I don't lose my instrument. My music does not suffer; I'll just offer it out to someone else. Where's the 'rejection' here? To say we are 'rejected' with a woman if she doesn't jam with us, would be similar to Mozart playing to a room full of people, someone walking out the concert hall, and Mozart slamming the piano lid down and storming off in a huff, "oh nein, ich wurde zurückgewiesen!"

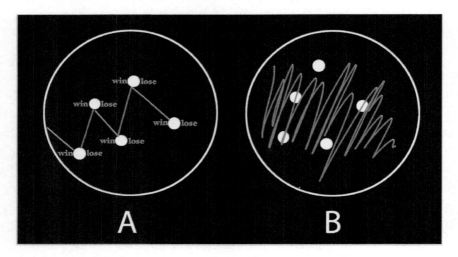

To summarise: In Circle A, you are 'approaching' each point and there is an instant win or lose on each one. In Circle B, you forget about the points and just colour in the circle. In the instances where you didn't connect with any points, you are not 'rejected', because your intention was just to colour in. Yet you still connected to some of the dots.

How to Kill Flow in a Second

Here's the thing. Once you impart and apply the concept of 'approach' and 'rejection' into your interactions with women, you snap yourself back into Circle A, back into the pick-up paradigm—back into judgment. You're now that rat in the lab maze. You have decided that it's possible to win or lose something. You snap back into a dualistic Work-Frame to force the required result and ultimately you stop being truly free. You are now in survival-mode and operating from a fear-based mindset again, where to solve this little pick-up problem, you need a pick-up solution and so the pick-up merry-go-round continues.

We're going to go into great detail on exactly how you can take steps to free yourself for good. This idea of interacting with the world with Autonomy is actually the simplest thing in the world but can be tricky to understand if we've been stuck in PUA Pleasure Island for too long. So, in the next chapter I show you examples in different social settings...

Academy Exercise

Whilst walking down the street...

1. Make eye contact with girls that pass by, but keep walking on

2. Make E.C, but now also smile, as you keep walking on

3. Make E.C, smile and now say "hi", but keep walking on

4. Make E.C, smile, say "Hi" but now stop as you say it, and start conversation

UltimateDatingProgram.com

Chapter 14 – Autonomy vs. Hunting: 3 Examples

Autonomy is a simple concept but it can be tricky to understand at first, if you are used to living life as a PUA hunter. So let's take a look at some examples, and how being masculine works from within that powerful frame.

We'll look at 3 situations: at a party, in a cafe, and alone walking down the street.

At a Party

I was speaking with a friend the other day, and she told me about these two Spanish guys she knows who go out to bars to do pick-up. They were at a private sort of underground party with a whole group of friends and good people. The atmosphere was a lot of jumping and a bit of silliness, and everyone was having a shitload of fun. Just playing, being silly, loving life. Guys and girls.

These two Spanish pick-up guys were just standing by the wall. They couldn't relax and play. Their minds were locked in Work-Frame pick-up mode from so much hunting.

They simply couldn't relax and see the venue as a place to let go and play. They needed some sort of outcome. I think we all know those two guys—we've been them!

So let's say in a party environment, you were doing pick-up. You go in there and 'Game' the room and hunt like a shark, and don't have fun but you work away until the early hours. You have a small chance of having a good time, if you 'succeed', by whatever criteria you have decided. Presumably getting a number, a kiss, or sleeping with someone. Then, if you achieve one of them, for a moment, you feel a slight sense of ease.

In reality you've not created or enhanced any real relationship. You've made no new genuine connection with anyone. You've not been relaxed or real and consequently you're locked out of the moment. You're not even living life. You most likely experienced some form of anxiety or stress during the night. You were working. No play at all.

Now, let's look at the Social Artist at a party. You're there to have fun. Your priority and higher purpose is, naturally to have a great laugh with your friends and making new friends. You are full of

101

excitement, just playing, joking around, uplifting the people around you and being uplifted. Making some great connections and having some great interactions. You are expressing yourself to everyone including the women there. With your unbridled sense of play, you connect with them. Perhaps you meet a woman who is also attracted to you; you talk, joke and express some saucy vibes. You invite her to play with you, by leading her with the gift of your masculine attention and intention. This creates a magical *tension* between you.

If she walks away to chat to other friends, you instantly dissolve back into your original purpose of having fun. You're not pretending, you really, truly are having a great time.

The Social Artist is 99% focused on what they're already doing. And then gives 1% to a woman, but within that 1% they give their absolute all, because it's just spilling a bit of the fun-lovin' out from their 99%. It hardly matters what happens with that 1%, it's just a gift, an invitation. That's all.

But a pick-up artist goes 'all in' with his poker chips. He sticks all his eggs into one basket. He sticks his nuts on the chopping block every time he 'approaches' his 'target' and seeks that 'close'. Of course he does, he's in survival-mode. Here, a pick-up artist is pretending to not be needy, but inside he is really feeling stress. He is thinking and strategising and working away.

You—the self-healed Social Artist—are so god-damned content because life is so good in that moment that you are a fulfilled person. You are with friends and making new ones. Inside this state of mind, you look up, think *'whoa, who's that girl?'* and go grab her to share the fun with her. Excitedly, you invite her into your already established bubble of play. You only want to create something with her. You have an urge to merge. She feels it. Everyone feels it. You're a gift to that party: a warm sun that engulfs everyone with its rays.

As for the pick-up artist at that party? Who is he? A black hole. He's there with an agenda. A dark, nasty, man-child who wants to take something from these people. With his mask on, he wants to step into their lives, and he wants to get his results from them at any cost using his arsenal of tactics—All motivated to relieve his lack-tension.

Now, picture the two different men at this party—one is a pick-up artist, and the other is a Social Artist. As they both do their thing, can you see the difference from the outside? Maybe, maybe not. If you watch them closely all night, you certainly will notice a difference. And believe me, women do. One is working. One is playing. One is taking. One is expressing. One is all about pain and escaping ego-death. One is sharing good vibes. For the pick-up artist, it's all about survival. The other is all about fun, connection and thriving in the moment.

Imagine a pick-up artist watching the Social Artist through his pick-up goggles—how would they see him?

Let's imagine those two Spanish PUAs are watching me (or soon, you) play. They might not be able to see the difference. They could see me playing and say "ah, he's getting in state" and then they see me giving a girl that 1% of my fun and attention unconditionally, and they say "ah, he's 'opened', now he's touching her arm, so he's 'kino-escalating' and now she's talking to someone else so he's 'rejected', and now he's kissing another girl so he just 'k-closed'. He's a 'semi-good PUA'."

PUA's have a very hard time seeing things in any way other than through pick-up and acquisition. Those pick-up goggles stay on tight. But now you are becoming an aware (and natural) person once more, and you can see the difference, can't you? Most of the significant differences are internal, but let's look at some more situations to illustrate.

Sitting with Friends in a Cafe

You are sitting in a cafe with two friends who all do pick-up or who are at least see interactions with women as acquisition. You're sitting, chatting and having a good old laugh. Then, a group of cute girls sit down on the next table. There is an immediate break in the conversation. Suddenly the autonomy is gone. Your eyes dart across to the girls. You start making little comments under your breath to each other. You say words like 'IOI', 'opener' 'locking in'. You have all stopped having fun together, and you are creating separation between you and the girls, by looking at them as objectives and searching for a way you can engineer a strategy towards a result.

Bingo, you're now in a Work-Frame.

Of course, you now have to 'approach'. Because actions from the Work-Frame creates separation and perceives these women as distant objects. Approaching is a way to bridge this gap you've created for yourself. You are preparing to hunt them. To begin a sequence of strategic actions until you hopefully 'close' one of them and escape ego-death for a moment. Then on to the next girl. Work, work, work. Survive, survive, survive.

The women sitting next to you are almost irrelevant. Just targets, random enemies to be defeated, walking vaginas. When they sat down, you were already connected, but by switching to hunt-mode, you and your wingmen created an arbitrary barrier between your two groups, as you decide they will become your goals. These girls will now be on the receiving end of your lame acquisition strategy.

As the three of you turned your attention to picking these girls up, you instantly snap out of the relaxed playful mood you were in a moment before. You now have a job to do, with high stakes. You start to feel stress, and think about how to manage that stress. You try to calm yourself as you think of a good 'opener'. An opener for God's sake—what is she, a can of beans? Fort bloody Knox? She was never closed to you in the first place! Just saying 'opener' means you have to open something that is closed. You are just telling yourself that she is closed to you.

Ok, now let's look at three Social Artists: natural, healthy masculine men. They are having a great time in the cafe. Then, the girls walk in and sit down next to them. You don't for a moment stop having fun with your friends. You are joking, laughing, or talking about whatever you were before.

You're in a bubble of play, naturally. You are fulfilled and in a higher sense of purpose beyond women— having a good time with your friends and enjoying the moment.

You notice the girls and you may feel you want to invite them into your bubble of fun. You offer an invitation to the already established play you are having, and they may or may not respond. You offered out because you are comfortable with your masculine expression and you simply felt like it. If they ignore you, does it matter? In the very same second you are still talking with your friends again, lost in the fun you were *already* having. Perhaps you will offer yourselves out to some more guys and girls you meet later. Of course you do, that is how you live.

So, as a Social Artist, what happened there with the girls? If they didn't click and chat with you, did anything happen? No. Of course not. Nothing happened there at all. You invited, that's it. Seamlessly and with no judgment around your actions, you dissolve back into your original purpose, your autonomy—your 99%. The bubble is unaffected. You are able to give offerings out to people all the time because you are so relaxed and content within yourself, that you just want to spill it out. Women love it. Most people love it.

105

Let's look at the group of pick-up guys in that cafe. They are not inviting, because they have nothing of any intrinsic value to invite into. They don't invite, they 'approach'. They are coming from a void space that needs filling. They are grasping for girls (after building up the courage and wrestling with their growing 'hunter's anxiety') and the girls respond well to their 'opener' and they are in. Onto the next step in the strategy, up the acquisition ladder, where every rung on that ladder of 'escalation' is a potential place to fail.

Or let's say those girls don't respond well when you try to 'open' them. What happened there? Because you're doing pick-up, you tell yourself you got 'rejected', which is because you've accepted all these limiting rules. You've attempted to acquire and you failed. Just like the rats in the maze, you all feel a bit of a sting, and console each other.

Let's see how different they look from the outside. Can you picture them? One group of fun-lovin' guys are autonomous, content, fulfilled. They are having fun and immersed in their own activity. They have something appealing to invite women and other guys into when they feel like it. The pick-up guys, on the other hand, are trying to survive, and they are acting to cover up their lack tension. They are constantly trying to bridge the gap between one object (themselves) and another object ('the target').

So, can you see the difference from the outside? Maybe, maybe not. It can be subtle unless you watch closely for a long time.

The three questions you must ask yourself are these:

1. Which type of man do I want to be?

2. Which group of friends do I want?

3. And put yourself in the women's shoes for a moment. Which group of men do you think they want to meet and enter into their lives with?

Walking in the Street During the Day

Now, I get a lot of people asking me "what about when I'm alone? What if I'm not with my friends, not having fun, and seemingly not doing anything. Where's my autonomy then?"

When you're alone, you always remind yourself of the purpose of what you are doing and where you are going in that moment. That might be going shopping, on the way to the gym or enjoying a stroll around the park.

On a deeper level, you always fall back into who you are as a man and where you're going *in life*. In other words—your life's purpose that makes up your identity. Falling back into who you are as a man, in a way that is unwavering and internally validating is the alchemic pinnacle of autonomy. When you move from *doing* autonomy, to genuinely *being* autonomous in your life and being comfortable in your own skin, is when you have truly arrived as a man.

In pick-up terms they may consider this 'inner-game'. But in reality there is no gaming, inner or outer in a Social Heartistry paradigm. This is about having the high self-esteem and self-worth, that comes with knowing your own importance and impact in the world, and therefore no woman's reaction to you, will ever negatively affect you. That's power.

Let's play our little visualisation game again. Picture first, the Day Gamer on his own scouring the streets. He is on a mission to find a woman. He is hunting in the clearest possible way. He needs a result. He is battling with all sorts of inner mind games to control the hunter's anxiety and creepiness that is rising up in him. He tells himself he has to 'open' ten girls to warm up.

Then he'll start getting numbers and instant dates. He's walking around looking for 'targets', stopping them, gaming, closing, getting rejected a lot, because that's all part of The Game, right? He's a stressed out, isolated man-child without any love in his heart for any of the people he is meeting. He is trying to survive another day of impending ego-death by acquiring results.

Now, the Social Artist. He's strolling down the road, enjoying whatever he's doing. He is 99% immersed in the moment and what is happening around him. He is a fulfilled man. Perhaps he is going somewhere right now, perhaps he is just strolling. Or perhaps he feels into his higher purpose. His life journey and he is feeling good and so he feels like giving and spreading this good feeling.

A gorgeous girl walks past and in that moment he feels like expressing himself to her. So he stops her and does so, just spilling out whatever comes out spontaneously in that moment. He only has playful intentions in that moment. He just wants to express and share his curiosity for her. Giving her the gift of his masculine edge with child-like curiosity and wonder.

They don't click? She doesn't accept his invitation? Fine, he happily strolls on. Still completely grounded in his original purpose. He was winning before, and continues winning without her.

If she does accept his invitation, that's fine too. Because he is within his masculine, he expresses it by leading her to a bar or cafe. A true adventure is beginning. Who knows what will happen next?

See the difference? Can you feel the difference? Once again my friend, which one do you want to be?

Live, Breathe, BE Autonomy

As I write this, I'm in a bar. The music's groovin' away. The atmosphere is great, it's like a cosy hipster vibe and of course a guy with a hipster beard is scratching on vinyl and there's a hipster dog milling around. It's one of *those* places. I'm sat on a big vintage sofa. My bigger purpose right now is writing this book for you.

There's a girl in her late 30's who's covered in tattoos. She's quite foxy, and she is playfully dancing around me. I throw out comments and observations about her dance moves! Sometimes she receives what I say, other times she's in her own world. Sometimes she goes around the bar to talk to friends, and sometimes she's back near me. I playfully command that she sits next to me to give me a cuddle. "Hey come here girl, gimme some sugar!" And I pull her down next to me. She laughs gives me a cuddle and jumps back up to dance.

Whether or not she jumped down to give me cuddle or not, it's cool either way, there is NO pick-up, NO 'approaching', NO Game, NO 'rejection'. But there is still potential and possibility for an embrace, for connection, for intimacy, for fun. Christ almighty, it's so awesome to play this way. Two free Social Artists with the playful hearts of children, sharing their fun and play with each other. That's right, she is also a Social Artist... Go back and read what I said about how she is interacting with the bar.

We are two people in the flow of life. Who knows what will happen later? I am loving her company and will keep expressing myself to her and having fun with her. And she will most likely keep on expressing herself to me too. We might end up at home together. We might end up meeting another time. We might become friends, lovers. We might never see each other again. But would that be rejection? Fuck no. What a ridiculous idea.

Academy Exercise

Whilst in your 99% purpose, stop 3-5 girls and express your interest in her. If at any point she is not interested, simply wish her a great day and go back into your 99%. See if you can focus so much on your 99% that this girl's reaction has NO effect on you whatsoever.

UltimateDatingProgram.com

Chapter 15 – Principle #2: Giving (Unconditionally)

When you're going out to *get* girls and you *get* 'rejected', you've lost. That's it, you're out The Game—it's Game Over.

But the shift in mindset—the paradigm shift here; is now we're going out and we're just expressing and giving ourselves away unconditionally.

When we see a girl we like, we're serving her, we're serving ourselves, we're serving the moment, yet at all times it's unconditional. That might be kind of hard for some of you guys reading that, because you're thinking: *"I want them, I need girls!"* You may be going out solely to seek 'results'. Well, that's part of your evolution. That's part of the process of reaching an unconditional stage where you can:

- Express your intent

- Let go of any fixed outcome

- Fully participate and lead decisively

- Still be fulfilled and in a continuous, purposeful flow

This is totally unprecedented. No one is speaking about this in modern dating advice. And you know why—because dating advice is placed in the same bracket as "GET rich quick" and "how to GET success".

"How to GET laid" is the snake oil that sells quickly, especially guys deep in pain and whilst this may appeal to your logical mind, to apply this way of interacting around women, will only make you repellent.

The Path to Liberation—Giving Unconditionally

In the first story in Belgrade, Serbia—I was leading with control and trying to take. In the second example I was leading with freedom and a willingness to create. There was no attachment to outcome, and I was giving from the inside out. I wasn't giving on the surface level, as a strategy to seeking sex. If so, then it would have become a pick-up strategy in order to acquire (in other words: giving to get)

I had *completely* freed myself from outcome by inverting the intention on the street from taking to giving. As I felt into the beautiful gift I was about to give, it wasn't about me anymore, and the need to fill my hole. I was freed from fear and became fulfilled in the very action I was participating in and yet I was still able to create an incredible romantic adventure.

I once had a student that said to me:

"John, I did what you said, I was with a girl and she was cold, so I gave her my jacket, but she wouldn't fuck me. I did that giving stuff. What went wrong?"

Here you can see, he was giving on the surface, but he was giving *conditionally*. He was giving to get.

112

How to Know if You are Truly Giving or Taking?

To get this clear, you must break GIVING and TAKING down to its two component levels—the action level & the intention level:

Action level—this refers to the actual physical action. Such as buying someone a drink, or putting your jacket around a girl, taking a girl by the hand, kissing, leading. It is everything you can observe happening physically.

Intention level—this is the true intention and core motivation behind the action. In the instance before where the student gave his jacket to the girl, from the action level he was indeed giving. However, his actual *intention* by giving the jacket was to eventually take a return from the girl in affection. The moment you keep score, you are subtly investing, which becomes an intention of taking—just a drawn out version.

You will know when you're doing this. You feel it inside. Let's illustrate. In pubs in England, here's a typical scenario:

"Hey John, what do you want to drink?"

"I'm ok mate, I don't want in on around".

Oh shut up you tart, I know you're ok, but what do you want".

"Ok ok, I'll have a pint".

30 mins later…

"Your round John".

This offer of a beer is a subtle code of reciprocity disguised as unconditionally giving and nice guys do it all the time with women.

With the example of the student giving his jacket, he was investing with his motives.

Much like when we go into our local coffee house and we get the loyalty stamps. I'm on my 9th stamp so when I get my 10th stamp I'll get my free coffee. Guys giving *conditionally* are trying to stack credits with the girl so that eventually she will feel obliged to offer something back to him, in the form of a pity fuck.

"I've given her my jacket, bought her dinner, and drinks, maybe now I've worn her down enough".

In this way, his true intention was taking—just with the action level of giving built into the strategy. I don't need to say it but don't be that guy. This is not the giving I'm talking about.

GIVING via Taking

Let's flip the script here. If you are holding a piece of rubbish in your hand and I TAKE it off you and put it in the bin—I have on the action level TAKEN. However, my intention is GIVING you the freedom and convenience of not having to hold onto it anymore. Therefore, my core intention is I am GIVING even though you could say I TOOK from you.

I often receive a text from my friend "Hey, how are you mate?" On the action level this looks like he is giving—since he is being friendly and seeing how I am. However, I normally sigh and ignore texts like this because I feel my energy is being sapped because of an obligation to respond with something *more* interesting.

In fact, I'm sure everyone reading this, has one or two texts in their phone right now which they have ignored as a result of a similar lazy text. You consciously or unconsciously know the intention of the text is; "I am bored, entertain me". (TAKING)

When you go into an interaction with women you should be intentionally GIVING. Not 'giving value' as another pick-up technique to acquire (giving to get). But, GIVING an invitation of you to them, without attachment. Expressing unconditionally. And be totally fine with any eventuality, because you're already doing something.

You are giving your curiosity, your desire, your power, your play, your masculinity, your sexuality, your emotional intelligence, your attention to them. You open yourself and give. Not in a material sense but as the playful child that loves to express and play with everyone for the sake of playing.

With women we like, it comes from a potential to create intimacy and adventure with her and it isn't dependent on her reaction. It's an offering, a gift. We feel it and we give. When we allow ourselves to do this *unconditionally*, we give out a totally different 'vibe'. This represents to women a much higher perceived emotional gain, and they often become attracted.

Here's the thing—the moment you keep score and say; *"I'll give, but only if it'll work"*, it's no longer unconditional and now you're back in pick-up again—you're in a Work-Frame. You're needy.

Intentionally Giving (Vibes) and Physically Taking (Leading)

The less a guy needs something, the better he can give. He's the one that emits good vibes and he can then invite girls into his reality. He can continue this gift by pulling her in for a kiss, and even doing this very decisively and dominantly (physically taking) but the overall intention is one of joint adventure (intentionally giving) and therefore she feels that action as a gift.

You can watch me demonstrating this on the **Ultimate Dating Program**, where I see a girl dancing next to me on the dancefloor and I tap her on the shoulder, she turns round and without any words or preamble, I twirl her straight into a snog. All within around 5 seconds.

When the above situation happens, it is like a rollercoaster ride for her. She can feel that the man does not need the kiss like a starved animal needs food. He is autonomous within himself and is fulfilled by the very playful process of it. It creates emotional contagion, where she feels the good vibes that he is emitting.

When I walk into a bar and I feel good, girls can already feel my good vibes, and when I invite her in towards me, this is amplified. When I'm talking to her, listening to her and leading things she can feel this as a huge gift.

Conversely, when I feel low, due to various reasons which are all part of being human; a break up, a death, bad news, a hangover— I can slip back into black-hole mode (pick-up mindset) and I look to take from others because I feel empty and need comforting. YES, that still happens from time to time such as when I did the European tour the second time remember?

When I feel this Acquisition Work-Frame setting in, I often say to myself;

"Johnnnnn, don't be so selfish, you don't own this woman, she's not yours to have!"

All I can do is express to her and give her my *Hadouken* of play and desire. And if she wants to do some sexy sparring with me and throw back some Chun-Li flying leg kicks and we get into a sexy tussle then all good in da' hood. If not, I'm unaffected. That's the embodiment of a Social Artist.

In my PUA days I used to go out and get girls numbers thinking I was da' man. It was coming from a place of ego-massaging and validation seeking (taking). Now when I go out, it's coming from a place of creating fun with anyone in my radius (giving) and because of this I can make a statement, without asking for permission;

"Hey, let me TAKE you for a drink" or "Hey GIMME your number" or "Hey COME with me".

Semantically, this might look cocky, controlling or manipulative but it's not, because on the intentional level it's about offering a gift to both of us. Co-creating an adventure together. She will feel this as non-neediness and she will find it attractive. You can then:

- TAKE her by the hand

- TAKE her up the stairs to the bedroom

- TAKE her clothes off

- TAKE her sexually

Notice how I say TAKE. But the overall intention is one of GIVING—giving her adventure, fun, danger, wildness, or simply an escape from the mundane...

She will feel the difference and so she should. Even when you ring a girl up and ask her out, if you're feeling needy, she'll feel it. Even if you pretend to be cool and detached using the PUA shield. She'll pick up on it. Even if she doesn't consciously, on some higher awareness she does, and she'll follow her intuition and flake on you.

If, however you are coming from an intention of creation without need, just an urge to share good vibes, you can be very decisive and somewhat forward and even say "I really NEED to see you!" and yet she'll interpret and feel that as non-needy, which is accurate.

Physically Taking—Taking Masculine Action

As I went down this new path, it got to the point where, if I wasn't feeling good in myself, I'd consider taking masculine action as being selfish. But this was a lesson to be learnt about my own self-worth.

Because in that moment, I didn't feel like I had anything to offer. I saw leading things sexually, such as pulling girls in for a kiss, as just taking. Once I realised my own value and what I was worth and what I was providing to people, the act of physically taking (leading) was now an intentional gift. Girls want me to pull them in for a kiss. They want me to interact with them with this masculine intent.

When you can combine the emotional impact of expressing unconditionally to a girl on the intention level combined with leading on the action level—that is when the magic happens. Think about when you twirl a girl on the dance-floor into a kiss. You're GIVING a fun energy, yet you are physically TAKING her hand and pulling them in. It is therefore received as a gift.

To the untrained PUA eye, the idea of giving appears like White Knight behaviour. It doesn't sound very badass. Giving in the sense I'm talking about isn't the PG kids' movie where Corey- the-pimpled- teenage- underdog sweet-talks the stunning girl off the cooler, harder kid by being a complete wuss.

I'm talking about giving as a core, visceral intention. You can have fun taking girls by the hand and pulling them in for a coffee or a glass of wine or up the stairs to the bedroom and at all times it's an offering, a gift.

So remember, leading from a place of control and Acquisition is taking (PUA). Leading from a place of unconditional creation is intentionally giving (Social Heartistry).

Academy Exercise

Try this simple yet powerful exercise to show the difference between taking and giving on an intentional level. Firstly, you are going to walk around and beg for a £1 coin from a stranger (use your own local currency). Keep doing this until you get one. Then, you are going to walk around and just offer the coin to passers-by. Notice how different you feel when people don't accept the coin, as opposed to when you are unable to acquire the coin.

UltimateDatingProgram.Com

Chapter 16 – Principle #3: Play

"You can't lose if you don't play the game"

Romeo and Juliet Act 1 Scene 4

Not bad, Willy! But there's an old Johnny Coops line that goes one better…

"You can't lose if you're truly playing"

The Play-Frame

I had a bunch of students with me, that I was coaching at a sea-side resort called Sziget in Hungary. We were drinking cocktails by a beach- side bar. I decided to play some drinking games. One of them was to go round the group and say a person's name that started with the letter the last surname began with. James Bond, Barbara Streisand, Susan Boyle. You get it. Whoever failed to come up with a name, had to do a forfeit.

Bence couldn't think of anyone and so his forfeit was to jump onto the main strip and find a girl to twirl and come back. He jumped up giggling and went up to the very first girl he saw. She ignored him but Bence had no time for time wasters, and seamlessly and with no hesitation or judgment, moved onto another girl who accepted the twirl invite.

When Bence returned, I asked; "Were you 'rejected' with the first girl?"

"What do you mean?" He replied bemused.

"Well, didn't you want her to twirl with you?"

"I suppose, but I wasn't thinking of it like that, I didn't even really pay attention to her reaction, I was having FUN!"

In that fleeting moment, Bence had collapsed the binary outcome response of 'win' or 'rejection'. He had transcended the pick-up Acquisition Work-Frame completely.

The first girl's reaction was insignificant and had dissolved into Bence's Autonomy, which in this instance was his *Play*. That was his reward. Even though, he was sent on a clear mission—the response from the girls made no difference, as there was no judgment around it. He was free.

Human Pyramids

A few weeks later, I was in Budapest and doing a talk about this very subject of a PUA Work-Frame vs. a Social Heartistry Play-Frame. As I was doing the talk and trying to explain this concept of play—I thought to myself, wouldn't it be fucking ace if I got the room to experience it. So, with that, I got the whole room on their feet and walked them out the building and onto St Stephen's Square, a couple of minutes walk away.

I broke everyone into four teams, gave each team a hat and told them to make as much money as they could by doing human pyramids. (The idea came to me in the moment!)

So off they went, and started piling on top of each other. As I walked around and watched each team, I noticed every single person had the biggest smile on their face. One team even broke into an impromptu dance. Some teams could only manage to get two layers of people. One team got four layers of people, with a small girl right on the top!

A team pyramid, whilst another team break into an impromptu dance

When I called the teams back in, they were all giggling and still had big wide grins on their faces from what was a really fun game.

"How do you all feel?" I ask.

"We feel GREAT!" They all replied!

I asked each team to show the money they had accumulated in their hat.

Two teams just had a few coins, another team unbelievably had about £30's worth of local currency and one team had only one coin.

I ask the 'one coin' team; "Did you lose? Are you rejected?"

Much like Bence at the beginning of this chapter, they all had a look of bemusement.

"Noooo! Of course not!"

"But didn't I ask you to earn money? In fact, you came *last*".

Whilst they had the intention to earn money for their human pyramid escapade, they were clearly so immersed in the PLAY of the activity that they genuinely didn't care about the money. The money was a bonus—a side effect.

Likewise, I asked the team that had won the game by earning the most money— How do you feel with all that money?

They all agreed it didn't really make any difference to them.

That's because, just like Bence's forfeit, they were all in a Social Heartistry Play-Frame. Yes, they had the intention to earn money, but their focus and their reward was clearly on the activity itself. Through play, they had collapsed the binary outcome options of 1's and 0's and could not lose. They were impervious to rejection. Yet they were *still* attracting money in their hat!

Working *for* Women or Playing *with* Women?

Since the PUA Game is there to be 'won', the community make their every move in order to win. Whatever is not done in the interest of winning is simply not part of The Game.

It's funny how we call pick-up artists 'players' yet they're working for a woman's affection. They've lost the art of play. Just as I had done in my early PUA days. Their success is rewarded only upon completion, so their conversations will always be transactional rather than interactional. Always work, *never* play.

So how do we know if we're working or playing around women?

- If you are feeling anxious around women, you are not playing, you are working

- If you are worried how you are coming across or how your body language is appearing, you are not playing, you are working

- If you are worried about what to say or how to keep the conversation going, you are not playing, you are working

- If you are worried about how she is perceiving you, or what others around you are thinking about you, then you are not playing, you are working

When you're with women, if they sense you working for them, they will be instantly repelled. Even if you deploy the counteracting techniques from the PUA shield to hide the neediness, such as pretending to be alpha, or being 'cocky-funny', they'll keep testing you until you eventually slip up and she'll realise you've been in a Work-Frame all along. This is in essence, what they refer to as 'shit tests'. She's sussed you out.

Also, when you 'score' someone concedes. When you get that close, with a woman, she loses. It may be subtle but on some level, she feels it and knows, just like my textbook pick up story.

"Why would I want to mess about and play when I want girls?"
Crowd comment from my 21 Convention talk in 2019

Here you can see this poor PUA chap is looking at play through the Work-Frame lens. He sees play as a form of 'messing about'. He's unable to see how play is actually a powerful form of creation. To him only setting a specific goal and working hard to achieve that specific goal, taking the straight-line approach, results in any kind of manifestation. Sad huh?

Let looks at the following example:

A **survivalist fisherman** lives on a remote island with no-one else to provide food for him. His *goal* is to catch fish. If he does not catch any fish, his whole family will go without food. He is now in survival-mode. He will now be desperate to control the outcome so that he guarantees that result and he either wins or gets 'rejected'. This is the Work-Frame in action.

A **recreational fisherman** on the other hand—His *intention* is to catch fish. However, the beauty of fishing for him is the whole ritual that surrounds the act itself—being out in nature, the sunshine, the stillness, the break from the city life. If, by the end of the day he hasn't caught a fish, he is NOT 'rejected'. He has NOT 'lost'. The fish simply become the bonus. He is winning despite the catch and so is always in a state of continuous winning. This is the Play-Frame in action.

From the outside looking in, the actions of both fishermen might technically look *exactly* the same, but the context is totally different.

125

One has a *goal* to catch fish and has immediately created the binary outcome response of 1's and 0's—win or lose. The other fisherman has the *intention* to catch fish but is rewarded through the play itself and can effortlessly embrace any eventuality, in one continuous flow. Ironically, he is *as* likely to actually catch a fish as the survivalist fisherman. I would even argue more likely, because he has let go of expectation.

Play is Moment-by-Moment Fulfilment

You see, when PUA's hear the word play, they assume it means goofing around and avoiding taking direct action. Maybe you're also thinking that, as you read this? But being in a Play-Frame, still involves direct action, it just means, removing any judgment or scoring based upon a fixed goal, and enjoying the moment-by-moment gratification, without any deferred outcome.

Take a salsa dance for instance, do you think the success comes from the very last step with your partner and then you pat yourself on the back?

What about listening to a beautiful concerto, do you think everything is geared up towards that very last clash of the cymbal. Or do you think the enjoyment was in every moment?

How about that crime mystery book? Did you only enjoy the book once you discovered "who dunnit" in the very last chapter? Or was the enjoyment in the reading?

What about that amazing 4 course meal you had, was the enjoyment on that final morsal of food you took into your mouth to fill your belly and quell your appetite, or was the enjoyment in the whole evening with your friends?

Work-Frame	Play-Frame
Porn	Tantra
Pick-up	Intimacy
Artisan	Artist
Engineer	Poet
Painting by Numbers	Painting
Debate	Dialogue
"Yes but"	"Yes and"
Survivalist Fisherman	Recreational Fisherman
Interrogation	Conversation
The Game	Games
Horny	Sexual
Actor	Improviser
The Worker	The Player
Pick-up Artist	**Social Artist**

How work and play differ in various contexts

Play is Intimacy and Intimacy is Play

Guys that are good with women, aren't the ones, in their heads, plotting what they're about to say next, and finding ways to engineer the interaction towards a definitive end point, they are the ones that are able to be unprepared and drop into the unknown and enjoy every moment with a woman, whilst still leading things. That's sexy.

An effective way to make that shift from working for women, to playing with women, lies in the following question…

When does sex start?

Ask any PUA and they'd say it starts the moment they get their dicks wet. It's a goal they need to hit and only when they reach their 'close' are they rewarded. But what if the sex began the moment you first made eye contact with her? How would this change the way you perceived the interaction and behaved within it?

Sure, the actual sexual intercourse is great, but when you're truly *with* a woman, is there any place the interaction *needs* to arrive at? If the act of sex is the only thing that can bring a reward to you, then the entire interaction is just prologued up to that end point. Wouldn't you say that's pretty damn unattractive to a woman as she's talking to you? Feeling that this guy, isn't present or content until he gets something later down the line from her.

Intimacy with a woman is different. It's moment-by-moment gratification. It is the Play-Frame in action. You tune in with each other and luxuriate in the enjoyment of *every* single moment.

Sex is intimacy and intimacy is PLAY.

Once you know that, and embody that, there is no rejection or pain of loss because your reward was the fulfilment that came within the activity itself. You can also keep leading and progressing the interaction into deeper levels of intimacy, whilst being fulfilled in every moment.

This is the fundamental difference between a horny guy and a sexual guy—one is working the other playing.

Players vs. Workers

You can see the difference between players living in the Play-Frame and workers living in the Work-Frame. When people go to a club for example—a play environment at its finest, the first thing most workers do when they walk in is 'approach' the bar to get a drink because they feel anxious and incomplete otherwise. Then they might go on the dance-floor—a crucible for play. The workers are those who are uncomfortable, looking around waiting for something to happen, or for 'targets' to 'approach'.

The players however are feeling the music and letting go. They are totally fulfilled and integrated with their environment—because they are playing. They spread their play around and invite people into their 'Play-bubble'.

Then after a while the workers feel awkward and unfulfilled, so they propose going out for a cigarette to give them something to accomplish.

By the end of the night, the players have had fun and go home smiling with or without girls. The workers, if they haven't achieved their 'result', go home with a kebab in their hand and an "I hate Night Game" expression slapped all over their Chevy Chase.

This is why I was assigned as the 'Night Game' specialist on the tours and it's why the other coaches were like a fish out of water in those environments. Applying their robotic Work-Frame methodology to a play environment like a club, is like fitting a square peg in a round hole.

Only those who are in the moment and playing, will be attractive.

Work-Frame	Play-Frame
Attachment to Outcome	Continuous Flow
Finite	Infinite
Win/Lose	Win or Win/Win
Defeating Opponents	Winning with Teammates
Deferred Gratification	Moment-by-Moment Gratification
Convergent	Divergent
Closure	Extended Play
Bounded by Time	Timeless
Limitations	Limitless
Rules	Suggestions
Transactional	Interactional
Goals	Intentions
Techniques	Principles
Controlling Objects	Exploring Possibility/Potential
Work Within Boundaries	Play With Boundaries
Binary	Superpositional
Rehearsed	Spontaneous
Complexity	Simplicity
Strategy	Presence
Approaching	Attracting
Controlling	Leading
Motivation	Inspiration
Contraction	Expansion
Expectation	Curiosity
Analysing	Awareness

Work Masquerading as Play

You may see PUA companies deploy 'self-amusement' or 'detachment from outcome'—concepts which refer to a genuine Play-Frame. But they're using 'self-amusement' and 'detachment' as techniques to reach that outcome. That my friend is work masquerading as play.

No matter how hard PUA companies try and adopt these concepts, they will always create a paradox because they will plug them back into their PUA Work-Frame. There is no avoiding it. Therefore

Giving (unconditionally) becomes 'giving to get', Play becomes work, and Autonomy becomes the PUA shield.

This is why I stress; you cannot upgrade Game to arrive at Social Heartistry. In the same way you cannot upgrade the old lady to arrive at the young girl. You can't go deeper into hate to arrive at love. You can't fuck your way to virginity!

So, whatever you do, don't straddle lanes. You'll only crash in the middle lane. Only a complete paradigm shift will be sustainable. So that means instead of the measure of success being geared around results with women, your new badge of honour is your fulfilment and sense of enjoyment and well-being, which must exist besides women. You then simply extend yourself outwards, express like an artist and invite her into the party!

Academy Exercise

Stand outside a bar or pub and as people walk in, tell them: "It's £10 to get in tonight". As they chuckle or scoff at you, and barge past you, were you rejected? Did you lose? Much like my coffee Barista story in the Remembering to Play Chapter, find other ways to play, so that you are taking action yet at all times in a Play-Frame.

UltimateDatingProgram.com

Chapter 17 – Breaking the PUA Spell, Word by Word

'ABRACADABRA' in ancient Hebrew means, 'I create what I speak'.

We know there is a shared behaviour amongst the PUA community. We know they are all out on streets and in clubs hunting to acquire. This is where the awareness of the community is stuck at. But why can't they make that paradigm shift like I did and learn to interact with women from freedom and play?

That's because PUA cunningly traps its community members into a consensus of acquisition. These are the rules and regulations of 'working' The Game—the game of trying to 'win'. Obedience to these rules and regulations and structure is what holds the pick-up prison together. Minds enslaved by rules are energetically frozen and they can't flow and adapt with freedom or creativity. They are locked into a Work-Frame of only two potential responses of 'win' or 'lose' — 1's and 0's in accordance with the pick-up rulebook.

This dualistic Work-Frame is held together through the **language** that is used. (Most notably 'Approach' and 'Rejection'). PUA bases its entire language on the scoring system generated from this Work-Frame. And so, by using the language of scoring, traps you in a Work-Frame way of thinking, and therefore behaving—killing the opportunity to interact in the most natural and effortless way available to you.

And how is this managed in the pick-up world? Am I saying there is a pick-up control system like a PUA illuminati, and out pops little David Deangelo from behind the curtain? No, of course not. To see how this works, let's begin by tracing PUA back to some significant causal moments.

Infield: Going to War with Women

'Mystery Method' is the collectivised thought forms of Mystery—the main progenitor of the PUA community. He laid out a lot of pick-up memes that we know today. He modelled out his (limited) system for seducing women from his own subjective (extremely left-brained) perception of the territory. Creating definitions for each part of his seduction process.

Some examples of Mystery Method are: disarming, targets, shot gun neg, sniper negging, obstacles, sets, kino escalation, C1 comfort building, A1 attraction building, and so forth and so on.

We also have a residual collection of memes from traditional sales talk about how we must 'approach', 'open' and 'close' people.

The military language of pick-up artists

We may think the language in this image above describes reality when it comes to meeting women, but it refers to the specific pick-up perception. It shapes and creates the reality of people who have adopted this worldview.

Here's the thing. This is not normal language my friend! This is military language. This is going to bloody *war*!

The budding pick-up artist clings to these concepts like a soldier clings to his weapons. And guess what, when we use and express military language, what do you think is the perception of women that this language is anchored to? Do you think it is seeing women on a level playing field and wanting to play and merge in an excited and loving way? Course not!

It is an unhealthy feeling of revenge and retribution. Wanting to get one over her and survive.

134

Similar language is used in nerdy MMOs like World of Warcraft, war games and real-time strategy computer games.

This lingo was passed on from person to person, and sufficiently replicated, as viral memes. It reached a level of critical mass where these military memes habituated and consolidated within the collective awareness (community) and were commonly yet falsely accepted as a description of reality. And guess what? No one questions them to this day.

When we are in Conflict with Others, we are in Conflict with Ourselves

I'll be brutally honest here. When my girlfriend broke up with me, I felt empty and separated from women, and the pick-up language made perfect sense to me. I felt pain and associated that with the lack of women in my life. As my lack-tension grew and repelled women they became further away and more unattainable. I frantically grasped and grasped and misfired. So of course they're now the 'target' and of course I have to 'approach' and 'disarm' this dangerous 'object' that is separated from me and holding back what I want. The language seemed like an accurate description of reality because it was in perfect correspondence with my feeling towards women and myself at that time—that of unresolved pain and a closed heart.

The effect this had was to put me into the same war mode as if I was on the front line. I was in survival mode. I didn't want to be defeated by another woman so I had to defeat her first. I had to overpower her will with my arsenal of tactics.

Women, instead of being my teammates, were now the opponent— the enemy…

Where's my wingman? SARRRRRGE!

135

The community held onto these memes, not because they are true, but because the groupthink mentality does not challenge them. This unified awareness or 'hive mind' is currently held in place by the acceptance and operational activity of these memes. As the community continues to speak these memes, they are unwittingly trapping themselves into the domain of acquisition and holding the PUA Work-Frame context in place.

Aldous Huxley wrote in Brave New World that the programming of the mind would continue through suggestion and punishment until...

"At last the child's mind is these suggestions and the sum of the suggestions is the child's mind. And not the child's mind only. The adult's mind too all his life long. The mind that judges and desires and decides—made up of these suggestions. But all these suggestions are our suggestions... suggestions from the state".

That's what these PUA memes are. They are suggestions, not descriptions. Words that we take for granted and think are describing the territory but are shaping our experience.

Over the last few years the pick-up community now uses less and less of these original memes. You may have noticed how you have stopped using the word 'sarge' or 'obstacle' or 'target'. It has slowly boiled and reduced down, and a lot of the original concepts have disappeared. This is because the community is slowly healing its individual and collective pain body and moving more into right-brain/heart-centred awareness; and because of that, the corresponding left-brain and fear-based memes are fizzling away.

But unfortunately, the entire paradigm at the root-level is based on acquisition, so the community will never be able to transcend the Work-Frame if they casually use *any* of the PUA memes.

Academy Exercise

Semantic Engineering: Make a list of all the current PUA memes you use to inform your actions.

After looking at these words, ask yourself "Would I use these words when talking with my friends or family, or a guy I just met in my local pub, by the bar?"

If the answer is HELL NO, then it's likely you are being trapped in the PUA Work-Frame by the language you're using. So do away with them!

UltimateDatingProgram.com

Chapter 18 – You Don't 'Approach' Your Mum in the Kitchen

"John, how else are we meant to talk to the girl unless we 'approach' her? I mean I'm over here, she's there, of course you have to approach, that's just a fact." **Crowd comment from London talk**

What these budding PUA's cannot comprehend, is that I walk up to girls ALL the time and am probably the most decisive person I know, yet at all times I'm never 'approaching'.

When they hear me say I don't 'approach', they automatically assume I don't walk up to girls. That's because these PUA's are so entrenched in their own map of the world that they cannot see any other way of looking at the territory. Their minds are so calcified, and the pick-up goggles are stuck on so tight, that they cannot see any other way.

They forget the word 'approach' no longer has the conventional dictionary definition anymore:

1. Come near or nearer to (someone or something) in distance or time.

   "the train approached the main line".

   It actually now takes on the pick-up, sub-culture definition which now means:

2. The initial act in a sequence of trying to pick a girl up (Work-Frame)

If approach just meant moving closer to someone or something, then surely a successful 'approach' in pick-up would be walking up to a girl and her slapping you in the face or ignoring you as we would have still successfully achieved the act of the 'approach'.

But clearly, by the pick-up definition, that is an unsuccessful approach, as we did not reap any sort of positive result and make our way up the acquisition ladder. That's why in pick-up there are 'approach coaches' to help.

I'm sure we can all draw closer to a brick wall, a tree, or a lamppost. We don't need any 'approach coach' for this. The difference is we don't need anything back from these objects, but we do from the girl in question. This is why the pick-up meme 'approach' creates a different context and creates all the baggage that goes with it.

By operating from the concept of 'approach' we heap a huge amount of expectation on ourselves and are now in a state of judgment on our actions, attached to this act of needing a positive result in order to win.

Let me ask you: Do you *approach* your mum in the kitchen?

No? But how else are we meant to talk to her unless we 'approach' her?

Imagine you've recently become an uncle and you haven't seen the little fella yet. He's a beautiful bouncing baby boy, you go over to him in the room... did you just do your 'approach'? I mean he's there and I'm here. Of course I have to do my 'approach'—that's a fact, isn't it?

It sounds absurd to use this word in this context because you're not in a Work-Frame of needing a result.

Therefore, when we see a woman we like, and we operate from the concept of 'approach', we instantly create a win/lose Work-Frame. We therefore create that expectation, so of course we have the hesitation.

Approaching or Inviting

Each word we use has a certain energy to it and works in a particular way. We feel it in our bodies as an energy/vibration. It either assists and liberates or paralyses and immobilises. We think we are only describing the world, but we are actually creating our experience.

Take a moment and let's do an exercise. I want you to feel into the word 'approach'. Feel it in your body. Let your body fill completely with that sensation. Let me guide you further:

"There's the 'target', you have to do your '*cold* approach'."

Take a moment to let any emotions that come up, just come out. Now say out loud or write down those feelings that arise.

Now, let's do exactly the same exercise. Imagine you see a beautiful girl walk past, and "you just can't stop yourself from INVITING her".

Feel into the word 'invite'.

Take a moment to let any emotions that come up just naturally flow. Now, out loud or write down those feelings that come up.

Can you feel the difference between the two?

You felt the energy of 'approach' what is that energy? It's a feeling of uncertainty and caution, isn't it? There's an air of sensitivity. You approach a bomb, you approach the edge of a cliff, you approach a crime scene, or that sensitive issue at work. It is a word associated with trepidation and fear. So, hey let's use it with women we find attractive too—smart idea!

I imagine a cartoon burglar with his empty swag bag over his shoulder, tip-toeing towards the loot. So when you state the word approach with a girl, yup—guess what, you take on those same feelings, it's not rocket science and in doing so, puts a stranglehold around you and limits you. Some other words that might have come up for you: danger, anxiety, paralysis, cringeworthy, sleazy. They are all relevant.

Isn't it funny then, that if we know that this concept creates these feelings in us, then why are we using this word to shape our experience with a woman? It's absurd.

What is Attraction?

I sometimes give money to the NSPCA, as I am attracted to them for the work they do. But when a NSPCA charity worker approaches me on the street, I instinctively dodge around them. There's something about someone coming at me like a pick-up artist that repels me. It's acquisition—the beggar energy. Isn't that funny though, it's still the same company. But one is attracting my money, and the other is trying to approach me and they repel me. People give willingly to charities they are attracted to, but they hate to be taken from, because they simply feel as if they are being 'approached' by an individual with an ulterior motive to take behind that smile and all that energetic banter.

Attracting is: "I have everything I need, so you can come towards me, like a magnet". Think about the word attract; it's not going towards something but actually drawing something towards you as if it had a magnetic-pull. Think about the sun and how planets are magnetically pulled into the sun's orbit; would you say the sun takes or gives? Does the sun approach and hunt? Is the sun full or empty?

Even when I'm walking up to a woman, I'm still grounded in my purpose, and the feeling of attracting and absorbing her into me, into my orbit. If she doesn't want to come into my radius, it doesn't matter; I just offer the invitation out to another woman. I can keep walking around and doing that—it empowers me and gives me energy. But as soon as you operate from the word 'approach', it's saying; I'm empty, I'm inadequate, I'm unfulfilled and I need something from this woman to feel complete and adequate. Therefore, instantly there's a win or lose attached to this interaction. And fuck, I don't want to lose.

This then is what leads us onto the next concept we need to change…

Academy Exercise

When you next go out with your friends to a bar, create a table and start inviting random people to it. Tell them you're creating a table for new people to meet each other. (I did this in Paris on a boat party and had about 18 strangers all huddle around a small table!) As you establish a table with a fun vibe to it, when you invite people to it and they say no, are you personally effected? Who's lost out?

UltimateDatingProgram.com

Chapter 19 – Approach Anxiety or Nervous Excitement?

It may be hard to grasp but 'Approach Anxiety' (AA) is not a description of reality. It is merely an interpretation, or perceptual label which has been passed around long enough that it virally spread and habituated to become a mainstay PUA meme.

The meme itself perpetuates fear and falsely holds men down into a certain emotional, physical, and psychological state, and then only the pick-up company's products and services can 'attempt' at resolving this. It's classic Problem-Reaction-Solution. Or you could say Problem-Reaction-Pick-up-Product-You-Must-Buy.

As a PUA instructor you want to sell a product, but you know no-one will buy it, so you elicit the problem in men, make them panic then shove your product under their noses. Very much the same as how computer software companies create viruses then sell their anti-virus software.

Get butterflies in the tummy and feel excitement around a woman?

"Buy the "AA Annihilator for just £699 today!"

"Overcome your Approach Anxiety, destroy it, blast through it"— presupposing and cementing into its audience's perception, that whatever feeling they had, is an adversarial one.

But there's a much easier way. If you feel those butterflies in your stomach before you talk to a girl, that's good! That's your biological signal telling you that you're attracted to this woman. It can become a complimentary fuel this way.

But by labelling it as 'anxiety', it demonises the sensation and therefore becomes a debilitating emotion that must be 'overcome' 'destroyed' or 'meditated through'. This meme habituates and consolidates within the hive mind of the community and locks them into only one way of perceiving the butterflies in the tummy and therefore taking action with women—That of survival and battling with fear.

Expectation Creates Hesitation

Let's take the pick-up example: You are on the streets 'sarging' and doing your 'cold approaching'. You are waiting on the side of the street like a wolf waiting for his prey. Your eyes move from side to side. You are building up 'Approach Anxiety'. You see the stunning girl walk past and in that moment you freeze. Your body fills with cortisol, and you know you should go and 'cold approach' her, but you're cemented to the spot. You have created an expectation and therefore a hesitation.

"C'mon blast through it," you say to yourself, "you know you'll be glad to have done it once you've done it". You start an internal dialogue—torturing yourself. "What if people see me and think I'm lame?" More Approach Anxiety, more fear. You are in survival mode—you have become a reptile!

Now imagine you are walking along the street with purpose, you are actually doing something and going somewhere. You see a girl drop her purse and she hasn't noticed, and you run up to her and give it to her. How much anxiety was there in that moment? Unless you have basic social issues—absolutely NONE!

"But we can't wait for a girl to drop her purse all the time!" They cry!

They miss the point. It's not the physical action that has to be replicated, but the same context of unconditionally giving without need for reciprocity. Once you can internalise this, you can simply walk over and externalise it by saying "hello", but it's no longer a rung on the acquisition ladder and coming from a place of taking for survival. All your actions and communication comes from this place of overflow and you simply continue to lead the conversation in one continuous flow.

Destroy Approach Anxiety or Embrace Nerves?

Imagine you and your friend are going on a rollercoaster ride. You love rollercoaster rides and live for it. Your friend on the other hand is petrified of them. As you are in the queue and about to get on the ride, you both get a similar rush through your body. You interpret that as nervous excitement, but because your friend is shit scared something bad might happen, he interprets that same feeling as anxiety or outright fear.

Part of your route to freedom socially, is your ability to distinguish nerves (nervous excitement to create in the unknown) as opposed to anxiety (fear of losing and getting 'rejected')

Remember that when we're in a state of fear, we look to TAKE to survive and conversely, when we need to take to survive we reinforce FEAR.

If you need to take, you *should* perceive it as anxiety! That's hundreds of thousands of years' worth of evolution trying to keep you safe. That's your body's natural emergency system in action! However, someone who is in their heart space and in a Play-Frame, will not be in survival-mode and thus won't interpret the sensation as adversarial. Love and fear don't co-exist.

When I see a beautiful girl, I don't label it as this or that. I leave it at the sensation level. I just know that my biology is telling me I'm attracted to her. Because I have emancipated myself from pick-up, and the core pick-up context of trying to take, I can allow myself to be outward orientated and express this sensation of excitement as a gift.

If she doesn't want to accept this gift and engage with us, it doesn't matter, I can just give it out to someone else.

Like the sun, I beam out a ray of sunshine and if she wants a suntan, then great! If she wants to stay in the shade, too bad for her but I'll just keep on shining.

Don't fall for the AA trick. Drop AA, along with all the other community-created meme-based problems. Drop pick-up and the acquisition Work-Frame altogether and you'll soon find this entire complex of self-created problems disappear on the breeze like a fart in the wind.

Academy Exercise

You will notice people on the street handing out flyers, usually for local bars and clubs. Grab a stack of flyers from them and hand them out to passers-by. You will notice some people accept the flyer, others do not. Are you rejected if they don't accept the flyer? Are you identified by their response? What if you were to hand out notes of money to people and they refuse—are YOU rejected?

UltimateDatingProgram.com

Chapter 20 – Seduction is Reduction

We believe complexity is the way to mastery. The more we learn, the better we'll be—This huge arsenal, this huge artillery and then we'll be ready. Or so we think...

I asked one of my clients to get me a beer from behind the bar. As he was walking off, I said:

"I've changed my mind. Can you approach the bar, work around the obstacles, lock in, wait till you get an IOA (an indicator of availability from the barman), open him with a statement of intent to buy, then transition into the order, and close?"

He started hesitating and panicking.

"OR you can just get me a beer!"

Look at those two examples. They are actually the same thing. You would have to do all those small incremental steps to come back with a beer, but which is easier, hitting those multiple checkpoints or "just getting the beer?"

Intellectual Analysis Creates Emotional Paralysis

Guys that get into Game end up tying themselves in knots, over-intellectualising and mechanising everything, exhausting their interactions by breaking them down into these sequential steps. Paradoxically, this is only creating more hurdles and increasing the amount of necessary checkpoints to hit and potentially fail at, like the lab rats getting electrically shocked.

The more you define and label something, the more boxes you create, the more you fragment and compartmentalise; the more you limit yourself. All you are doing is creating more semantic blockages inside your mind and paralysing yourself. It's like trying to clear the house of the mind, by throwing more and more bricks and mortar into it.

If you want to drop into an effortless, instinctive, creative flow around women, you have to drop all the PUA memes and labels, which are intrinsically linked to judgment and a scoring system and instead allow yourself to be guided by feeling, intuition and your intent. Stop working and start PLAYING.

You will move from trying to do a pick-up *on* women, to creating something fun and sexy *with* women.

Constructs Constrict us

At some point in your development, you must find ways to distil everything you've learnt. Moving beyond the limitations, identifications, constructs and beyond the mental masturbation. Simplification and reduction of information and theory into less and less so that you are set free.

That may seem daunting. It certainly was for me at the start, when the very thought of not being in control in an interaction terrified me. I went away and found more ways to keep the conversation going by learning 'chick cracks', and routines, even NLP. I then thought I was evolving by ditching these and using Natural Game techniques.

Whilst I was able to keep the conversation going more expertly, I was finding I was disconnecting with women and becoming more unattractive.

That's because techniques are a way to avoid the uncertainty that comes with stepping into the unknown. We don't have trust in ourselves or what's unfolding, and we default to tried and tested material to give us the best chance of surviving. This is why it's so alluring to guys with low-self-esteem, just as it was to me.

Attraction Between the Words, Not in the Words

Once you realise that there is a sea of potential and possibility flowing between you and a woman at all times, you can stop trying to be the 'do-er' and you let go of yourself and become an open 'door'. You allow your curiosity/intent/desire for her, flow through you and fill your body as a (+) charge.

You then only have to open your mouth, and the intent is felt. It promotes the (-) feminine charge within her and it cycles around between the two of you. *You* know that *she* knows what the conversation is *really* about, even if you're talking about the weather!

Once you both choose to tune into this, the momentary pauses and silence within the conversation aren't a moment of panic to fill it with more 'stuff', but actually an opportunity for you and her to go deeper into that magnetism together and luxuriate within it. Think about the moment just before a kiss for example. Why on earth would you want to contaminate this, by throwing stupid words into it!

Moving from Techniques to Principles

Are you at the stage where you're trying to memorise and rattle off all these various arbitrary techniques in your interactions and you don't really know where they all fit in? Just like I was at the beginning of my PUA journey. It's so much hard work isn't it?

Instead of learning 100's of techniques and trying to string it altogether, like an actor on stage working through his script, you simply come from the *umbrella* principle that governs those particular techniques, and then you can let go and allow everything to unfold accordingly.

Think about when you smile. What techniques are you using to smile? Are you thinking 'narrow eyes', 'stretch lips out', 'show teeth?'

Or are you just feeling happy on the inside, and as a side effect all the technical aspects of your muscles work together in unison to form a smile, without you thinking about it?

Now think about the PUA shield and all the various techniques used. Qualifying, Self-Amusement, Disqualifying, Active-Disinterest, Push/Pull, False-Time-Constraints etc.

These techniques are trying to surface copy the mannerisms of the genuinely autonomous guy who doesn't do PUA, who is self-contained in his own actions.

If a guy is autonomous in his daily life, he will naturally have limited time to see a new person he's just met on the street and will probably only have 20 minutes before he's got to see his friend or get to his gym class. However, instead of focusing on the principle of Autonomy, the PUA community extrapolate the surface level behaviour, and turn it into the 'False-Time-Constraint' technique, which is when you tell a girl you only have X amount of time before you have to shoot off, whilst you invite her for a coffee. It's a lie and all in order to give the illusion of Autonomy (whilst desperately seeking a result).

If a guy is autonomous in his values and boundaries, he won't pander to any woman either, he will naturally challenge her on what she says, especially if it seems immoral, pathetic, or uncouth. He does this naturally, because as a man of high self-esteem, he holds everyone he meets, up to a high standard and isn't trying to win over the people he meets. This is the fundamental difference between a nice guy who does whatever it takes for people to like him vs. a good guy, who is always real and doesn't care how people react to him.

The PUA community sees this good guy and instead of focusing on the principle of Autonomy, they model and surface copy this behaviour to create "Qualifying" "Negging", "Push/Pull". All the while hoping she'll like him.

If you go through *any* seemingly effective PUA technique, that pick-up artists champion, and show it to me, there is always an umbrella principle which it comes from. Show me any one of the dozens of fruits from the tree and I can show you the root.

The entire social and attraction process can be boiled down to just 6 principles and within these 6 principles, covers everything you need to know.

Lucky for you, I have found all 6 of them.

I have already shown you the foundation; Autonomy, Giving, and the Play-Frame.

The final 3 principles I cover on the **Ultimate Dating Program** are: Desire, Emotional Intelligence and Leading.

When you learn to live from these 6 golden principles, you will no longer be up in your head, painstakingly trying to cobble together a series of arbitrary routines, or even techniques—you are able to go up to girls and be totally unprepared, trust in yourself and trust in the unknown, and let things unfold and play-out naturally, whilst leading things decisively.

At that point you can…

"Take everything you've learnt, stick it in a box and just go back to being *you* again."

So why not reconnect with the immense social intelligence you were born with. Throw out the toxic ideas of 'Game'. Declare Game Over and reclaim the life of social freedom and endless play you've always had inside.

Academy Exercise

Go out and find ways to interact with girls using your own unique style and identity. Perhaps you have a quirky silliness about you, perhaps you are very low energy and relaxed – own it. As the Social Artist your style is unique to you. Don't be a photocopy of someone else, be a limited edition of YOU!

UltimateDatingProgram.com

Chapter 21 – The Beginning

If everything I've said has begun to sink in, you are ready to make that change. You are ready to step out of the adolescent wastelands of pick-up. It's time for you to unplug from Game and step into your manhood. Your power. You deserve it for yourself.

No more Day Hunting, Night Hunting, Natural hunting, Inner-Hunting… Just stop Hunting! Drop all your wingmen; drop the military language, stop watching pick-up videos, get out of the forums and lairs.

Focus on your autonomy, your purpose. Heal yourself from within. Find balance aside from women whilst still interacting and leading women. Fully participate with the world, full of passion. Express unconditionally like an artist.

'Pick-up' your heavy heart, 'disarm' yourself, 'close' the old chapter. Not only will you be ready, but from this day forward, you will be free.

From the heart,

John Cooper

The Ultimate Dating Program

Do you resonate with my journey and message? Are you ready to escape PUA Pleasure Island? Do you want to go deeper with my teachings as a new blueprint for life?

Since 2015, I have been busy filming with CEO of Menprovement.com Sean Russell, on capturing this way of life and showing how Social Heartistry creates infinitely more connections and romantic adventures, as well as making you strong, creative and purposeful in your daily life.

I've filmed 40+ high definition videos in live social settings, such as clubs, dancefloors, parks, on the beach, on the streets, in cafes. All showing how to apply what I teach directly with the people around you, and create your own romantic adventures.

If you think you're ready and want to be part of a small band of brothers on the academy, with me John Cooper, by your side, where you get tutorship on all the Social Heartistry principles, including homework exercises, instructional videos and direct access to me, then head on over to my academy…

www.ultimatedatingprogram.com

Testimonials

1 hr

I'm an asshole. I was part of a Residential with John back in February and I haven't even let the rest of the world know what an awesome mentor John is. There was a lot of crying, a lot of hugs. John is one of the most compassionate people I have ever met, and that's not an exaggeration.

What you will learn is what he's preaching here: you WILL find your inner child again and you WILL realize that life is actually really simple (and that includes meeting women, tons if that's what you desire)... we just insist on making it complicated. Thank you again, John.

Of course, the work is not done once the Residential is over. What I learned since February: your physiology (the way you stand, move, breathe) dictates 100% how you feel and act.

For ALL the questions you have, the answers are already inside you, you just have to learn to ask the right questions.

Incantations (not autosuggestions) will rewire your brain and the way you see the world.

I have so much more to say and to share, but for now know that if you're struggling with yourself, with your dating life, and you want to handle it in a HEALTHY way, John is your only right bet.

Sorry for my English btw, I'm from Germany.

Hey guys, if you're reading this then
well done for having the balls to accept that
you want the best quality of women in your life
rather than having the left overs on a
Friday/Saturday nights!!! John has shown what is possible by
being yourself and having the belief in yourself. However its a
two way street and John expects you guys to do his
and your HOMEWORK! This homework is critical and by doing it
you will see the results coming together nicely. This is a small
solid group all looking to gain the same goal and will become
you're support network. P.S I forgot to mention the bonus its
MEGA cheap compared to any other PUA bootcamp which I have
been on before and trust me they are not the way to getting long
lasting success with beautiful girls!!! Enjoy the Adventure lads.
Dannie

Dude I just wanted to share this with you. I just can't believe what happened this weekend.

I was in Oxford. Saw this gorgeous girl walking on the high street. Went up to her, started talking. With in 10 minutes she was with me in a bar. She was a French tourist and it was day time, around 3pm. With in 20 minutes of our first interaction her tongue was in mouth.

Later in the evening she came down with me to Reading! Spent night with me and the sex was great! I just dropped her off at the train station. She is so far the most beautiful girl I have been in my life. I know it is just beginning but I can see light on the other side of the tunnel. Many Thanks to you dude.

Looking forward to catching up with you and our gang once you are back.

Sameer

Hey Johnny, just a short belated big THANK YOU for everything you did for me on the tour. It really has left an indelible mark on me. Im loving the hat, I've changed jobs and have put on some weight! Every day I think about the tour and cant help but get a bit sentimental about such a raw and unique experience. One of the main things I took away from the trip that has helped me a lot was your notion about fun, how nothing bad can happen if you go in with the mindset about fun. It really was one of the best things i've ever done and its hard to describe all the little ways it's made a big difference. I've got a new confidence and it feels like i've been through an initiation ritual into the rest of my life. Thanks again man, so many memories, your one of the best blokes i've ever met, i'll keep you updated and might even get skype going one time, hope all's well over in old London town!

Rob OM

Smörrebröd Römtömtöm ▸ John Cooper's Community

24 October

2016 is almost over and I want to thank you, John, for helping me make massive progress this year. This one week in Thailand in February has helped me more than anything I have done in the 5 years before.
Since I left Thailand I have lost a lot of weight and I'm basically in Fitness model shape, and I have met and dated a couple of really awesome girls. The biggest change, however, has happened in my head. I am so much more relaxed now, I see the abundance everywhere, not just when it comes to girls. The neediness is gone, completely. I can honestly say that, even though I may WANT to meet a certain girl, I'm not bummed out if we don't connect or it doesn't happen for other reasons.
It has been a long time since I felt like the universe is actually on my side.... so, thank you. Keep doing what you do, you're doing the world a great service.

 15 May

Wow crazy experience last night. Got invited to a house party which was alcohol free but had unlimited kombucha on-tap. Party kicked off with group meditation. After the meditation, I felt so integrated, like the whole universe was in that house and I was connected with everyone. Went to use the bathroom and saw a girl sitting at the stairs. She had such an attractive inviting energy so I said "hi, I saw you and felt this rush of attraction come from my chest" and she just smiled this beautiful smile and held eye contact. We didn't say anything at all for the next 3 min, just holding eye contact and smiling at each other. I then felt compelled to put my hand on her chest and feel her heart, and when I did, she did the same. I closed my eyes and we stayed like this for a minute, then hugged for probably another 2 minutes. Felt like I was soaking into her like rain. I kissed her on the forehead , said 'let's take a seat' and sat. We sat and held hands just looking at each other, smiling and just bathing in the moment. We kissed, then just continued holding the space. It was like we were having this whole conversation without words. Felt so honest, raw and beautiful. I'm so grateful for this course and the teachings, to allowing me to experience that moment through the principles of social heartistry. I feel like the way I'm moving through the world is totally different now. Fkn loving this!

👍 Like   💬 Comment

Guys here are four reasons why you need to enroll on this course :
1 - John is a genuine honest guy, who wants to help you to develop
and grow. This is his main motivation - not money. 2 - After around
30 seconds of watching him "in field" you will realize that he is
exactly who and what he claims to be. 3 - You don't have to rely on
or remember any rigid, mechanical pua routines. The emphasis is
purely on you to be your best self. 4 - It really works. It's as simple
as that. Adam

Do you realize what you have done, John?

Alexandru
to John ▾

Dear John,

It is not about the girls, not about attraction or how to make them want to have sex that I have learned these days. I
learned to let go and by doing that I am more and more free. I am afraid I will not recognize the place that I am
returning to, I will not recognize the city that I've been living in for fifteen years because now I see the world
differently. I now feel like writing poetry and music about what I feel when I meet women, John! This might actually
be the thing that I was telling you is missing from my unfinished songs. Read these lines about how I felt when I met
Katia from Ukraine at Starbucks this morning:

"You are Vienna, I am Budapest."

You are elegant, stylish and polite.
I am a bit dirtier but raw and intense.
Nothingness now starts to make sense
You are Vienna I am Budapest.

...

The actual words or quality of the expression above is not important just as the fact that the outcome when
interacting is not important. What is important is that it comes from Truth.
Do you realize what you have uncovered? You have opened something for the world to benefit. I will teach your art
through music, poetry or whatever form of expression I might find can better deliver the message. I want others to
see what I see.

Cheers
Alex.

Hey everyone. Just wanted to say that I actually met up with John last weekend in Budapest and got a few hours of instruction in the ways of Social Heartistry. Like a lot of guys, I studied pickup starting with "The Game" and found it to be largely artificial and dissatisfying. I eventually gave up on it, but still had been searching for a way to bring my true self without fear in social interactions, especially with women.

Since I'm fairly spiritually minded, I had often heard of the concept of "speaking from the heart center"...something which sounds real nice, but was also a little too abstract. I didn't know how really to put it into practice. John put me through some very practical exercises which showed me exactly how do it. All I can say now is that I feel like a completely different person. I no longer feel stress or fear when interacting with women that I find attractive. Nor do I feel as self conscious in social settings. Once you truly start coming from the heart, your only regret will be that you haven't been doing it earlier. This is some truly transcendental, life-changing stuff, and I highly recommend Johns course to everyone. If everyone practiced Social Heartistry, the world would be a much better place. Jacob x

Lately I've been thinking about unconditional love, how to spread it and how to use it in relation towards meeting women. Because I understood the concept of giving unconditionally, but I did not feel like I was doing it when I was meeting women. I still felt like I was outcome oriented, seeking together number or ego boost from the interaction and the simple fact that I could walk up to a woman and start talking with her.

I found a nice example, a metaphor, that helps me understand and actualize it in the world.

Imagine being an artist. A painter for example. You are sitting in a park during a sunny day. You decided to paint a panorama of a river bank with trees and people in it. As you are painting, a beautiful woman sits down on a bench nearby to observe the nature. You are so captivated by her, her beauty, maybe her energy, maybe she intrigues you in a different way. You decide in that moment you want to paint a picture of her. After you are done, you are so proud of your representation of what you saw, that you walk up to her and hand her the painting. You are not expecting anything from it. You were just excited when you saw her and you transformed your inner reality and feelings into the painting and now you are sharing it with her.

In that moment you don't care about whether she will like it or not. Maybe you don't even want to know her answer. You just want to share what and how you feel. Afterwards, she might like it and talk to you or thank you. She might not like it as well. You don't feel nervous about sharing the painting with her because painting the picture made you happy already. What happens next does not matter...

You are like a painter in your daily life. Just except of the painting, what you hand to people around you is your energy and your inner representation of your feelings in that moment. The painting you are sharing is the energy you have, the words you share, and smiles you give.

Thank you John, this is life-changing stuff. Daniel W.

Just wanted to say.... the best thing I did to start shifting to this paradigm and ditching the pickup one (in case others haven't still done it) is quit any lairs (or stop using them) and wingman groups if you haven't already. Just like John says. DO IT NOW. I heard John say this, but I kept using them for a while. I thought I could use them a bit of the time, the guys are really cool, where else will I find guys like that lol. Amazing what your mind can do to stop you. And STOP using the language as best possible is the other important one. It really works. The third most important thing I did was I took time off "picking up" girls for a while. Now when I talk to girls again I get a nice fluttery feeling around my body but it feels genuine, not like "AA" or a numbed sensation from going up to every chick on the street. It feels like I'm vulnerable but the interaction is real not like I'm spamming girls in real life. If I use even a bit of the language or hang out with a just a few pickup dudes, the pickup language and paradigm comes back. Basically I'm going cold turkey on pickup and dropping it like the plague, so I can step into the new paradigm. It's like a ping pong match, the pickup words keep fighting to come back in my head. I find myself slipping those words out every now and then and cringe. But once I get into that unconditional giving vibe, even temporarily, I feel a MASSIVE difference in interactions with girls.

The other day I spoke to this girl on the street and I had no other intentions but to give her a compliment and leave. I was also about to meet a friend, but she was too cute not to give a compliment. The thing was she kept lingering after I expressed my thoughts to her, and so I stayed and talked to her. We both liked each other clearly. I got her number (with the intention to take her on a fun date to a bar and seduce her for both our benefits) the thing was that intention came as I was talking to her not before, big difference. It wasn't "planned." And as soon as I got hers, she asked for mine. That's never happened before to me from memory....She texted me first when I was busy hanging with a friend. Saying "Well you're pretty cute." Damn haven't gotten a txt like that in a while . I look the same I have from ages ago imo. Maybe I dress a bit better. But I think when I start to give, girls start to see me as less needy and get more attracted to me and then they start to seduce me as well. they're getting a guy that isn't taking from them and instead enjoying the experience as it happens. It also is great because I never feel disappointed about a "bad night" (to do with girls anyway). And it feels like I'm just living my life and girls are popping in to my life and I'm hardly "trying" (even though I physically go up to them). It's a weird but awesome mindset shift.

brian naik

My story - I used to be the guy that always talked about girls, but never got any action. I'd go out to a bar and just hang out with my mates, not speaking to any of the girls. Or if I did, I wouldn't know what to say and would get rejected. Then I wouldn't talk to any more that night. I felt like a loser. But I'm not ugly, poor, lazy, unintelligent or unsuccessful. I just lacked something. John's course gave me what I was lacking. I'm now more confident than I ever have been with women and having loads of fun. I wouldn't have believed it was real, but the results are proof. Last week I hooked up with the girls I've been in love with for years... amazing! The best thing is that I'm not trying to be someone I'm not. I'm just me, but the best me I can be... armed with the weapons and understanding from John the guru. Lads, take it from me... this course will change your life! – Prash

FAQ's

Does Pick-up/Game actually work?

Yes and no. It depends how you look at it. If you're someone that sits at home in your mum's basement playing X-box all day, never leaving the house, and pick-up was the only thing available to you, then of course it will work. Because through percentages, talking to 100 girls a day will obviously be better than not talking to anyone. (1 of those interactions may stick).

If you're asking in terms of—is it an attractive way to present yourself to women? Then no, pick-up doesn't work. You can go around with your arm outstretched and approach 100 people and beg for money. By the end of the day, you have a few coins. You could argue it works right? But would you say begging is a successful way of accruing and attracting money? Hopefully not.

However, if you compare begging, to the guy that sits at home doing nothing, then actually begging *does* work. Any framework which encourages action is always going to be more fruitful than one that doesn't. If you throw enough shit at something, it will stick. Up until this point there has been no other available framework for men to interact with women other than through the acquisition-based prism of pick-up.

But pick-up works. I went out, did it and I got laid

Here's a story from a guy I went to university with;

"Hey man this pick-up stuff works! I went out last night and followed it through from start to finish. It was textbook pick-up. I approached this girl, I did some assumption stacking, teased a bit, kino'd, built comfort, broke rapport, qualified, bounced her and then took her home. I was getting L.M.R (last minute resistance) but then I did the 'freeze out' and it worked, I banged her. God damn man pick-up works".

I later bumped into the girl he was talking about, as I knew her as well and I asked her:

"Hey I hear you met Dave the other day and you had a good night!"

Her: "Oh god yeah, my boyfriend had just cheated on me so I was out to get revenge on him. I was making eyes with everyone and your mate Dave came over to me. He was acting really weird and creepy and doing this 'stuff' on me but I wanted a fuck and I thought it might as well be him as he's come over, and he's hot. He was acting a bit weird, but I was drunk at this point and let him take me home. One minute he was showing affection, the next he was pretending to be too cool for school. It was weird and it was putting me off. But then I saw a picture on my phone of my boyfriend and I thought 'bastard', and so I fucked Dave."

Here you can see, Dave thought it was his pick-up strategy that worked but in actual reality it was the thing that was working against him. It was simply the taking masculine action that created the opportunity for him, and pick-up doesn't own that... any more than begging owns making money!

Is it ok to start off with Game then switch to Social Heartistry when I'm ready?

Well, that's what I did. In a way I'm grateful to have taken the long and painful path, because it's made me be able to see the PUA matrix and to write this book for you!

I've had students later admit, that they knew Social Heartistry was the way forward but were still intoxicated by PUA. One student even said "PUA is the necessary evil". Meaning he needed to go deep into it, to then understand it was self-toxifying, to then transcend it. For him it was a stepping-stone.

So, if you want to see it like that, then be my guest! All I'm saying is that there's such an easier more effortless, more attractive way to live your life, which will save you so much time, money and pain.

Surely Pick-up is good for guys. They're getting more confident and developing valuable social skills?

As I said before, if you're someone that's used to sitting at home, not doing anything, then going out and doing Game, you will learn loads. However, lets imagine one day I told you to go out and pick pocket 100 people on the street. So up to that point you didn't really leave the house or talk to women at all.

By getting out there and pickpocketing 100 people, you would learn about body language, timing, awareness, social dynamics, emotional intelligence, touch, spatial awareness, getting outside your comfort zone, overcoming anxiety and so on. It would develop you in a myriad of ways. But would you then turn around and tell everyone that pick-pocketing is the way forward, it's the best way to develop yourself as a man?

You might say, "but pick pocketing has developed me as a man! I've approached loads of women and I even got laid because of pick pocketing. It must be the ONLY way!" Can you see how this would be akin to madness?

Whilst there are secondary benefits to learning Game, there is such an easier more effortless way to take the same amount of action, learn all those same social skills and yet not be the social pick-pocketer!

How do I know if my coach is a PUA or coming from a Social Heartistry paradigm?

One simple test you can do, is if you hear your coach use the word 'approach' or 'rejection' then you know he's teaching you from the binary pick-up paradigm. They're still in a scoring mindset and still locked in that Work-Frame of hunting for results. They may even claim to be teaching Natural Game. But it's still Game.

There are very few coaches out there who can even comprehend this paradigm shift let alone teach it, so don't be surprised that they're still operating within that out-dated PUA frame.

What kind of students do you coach? What level of development do they have to be at?

I coach a wide array of people. From 76 year old virgins to Bavarian Royalty! I also coach men and women.

However, I would say my speciality is coaching men, especially recovering PUA's, how to make that shift and come from this new paradigm.

Also, I work well with students who have the fire in the belly and are not frightened to throw themselves into it. If you're someone too shy to go up and talk to a girl, then whilst I can still help you progress, I'd suggest coming back to me when you have that base level of confidence.

What coaching services do you have and where are you based?

I'm based mainly in London but also travel around Europe. I run residentials each year, where you can come and live with me for 3-5 days and you can live and breathe what I teach, with me closely by your side.

I can also customise coaching sessions, where I can come and coach you in your home city or you can visit me.

Failing that, I recommend you do the Ultimate Dating Program, as it's the closest thing to live coaching, at a fraction of the price.

Printed in Great Britain
by Amazon

84446905R00098